Tough Guy Wisdom II
Return of the Tough Guy

Alain Burrese

TGW BOOKS
Missoula, Montana

Also by Alain Burrese:

Books:

Tough Guy Wisdom
Tough Guy Wisdom III: Revenge of the Tough Guy
Hard-Won Wisdom From The School Of Hard Knocks
Lost Conscience

DVDs:

Hapkido Hoshinsul
Streetfighting Essentials
Hapkido Cane
Lock On: Joint Locking Essentials vols. 1-5

Copyright © 2011 Alain Burrese
Print ISBN: 978-1-937872-02-1
eBook ISBN: 978-1-937872-03-8

Published by TGW Books, a division of
Burrese Enterprises, Inc.
Missoula, MT 59801, USA

Cover design by Bryan Whitney.

Visit the Tough Guy Wisdom website: www.toughguywisdom.com

DEDICATION

The *Tough Guy Wisdom* series is dedicated to my wife, Yi-saeng, and our daughter, Cosette. If nothing else, I want to be their "Tough Guy."

INTRODUCTION

I grew up watching tough guy movies, and I have to admit, they are still my favorite genre. Of course I watch other movies, but my favorites are watching a tough guy kicking ass and taking names, righting wrongs, punishing those who deserve it, and most of all – saying the lines the mark the epitome of cool, those lines we remember, repeat, and identify with "Tough Guys."

I'd even repeat the lines for real once in a while when younger and frequenting various watering holes and doing my best to be a tough guy. After all, as an Army paratrooper and sniper, I had to live up to those tough guy role models from the silver screen. I even made up my own tough guy line that I used in a bar or two, "You ain't big enough, and you don't have enough friends." Yeah, I thought I was cool, just like my movie heroes.

I'll also admit, it was Rambo in *First Blood* that influenced me to join the Army, go the Airborne and sniper route, and almost re-up to put in a Special Forces packet. I got out instead, and was influenced by Martin Riggs in the first two *Lethal Weapon* movies to head to Los Angeles and apply for the LAPD. (Yes, one could say I let movies influence me too much.) After being in LA for a bit, making the hiring list, and then speaking with an Army buddy's dad who was a Los Angeles fireman, I decided that going to college was a better choice and decided against wearing the Blue in LA.

The *Billy Jack* movies influenced my interest in the martial art of Hapkido. Many people remember this line from *Billy Jack*, "I'm going to take this right foot, and I'm going to wop you on that side of your face. And you want to know something, there's not a damn thing you're going to be able to do about it." At the time, I never knew I'd eventually live and train in South Korea, teach, write about, and do

DVDs on Hapkido, and have the opportunity to train with Grand Master Bong Soo Han, the Korean Hapkido master who performed the actual kick after that famous line. That was definitely a tough guy movie that influenced me in a very positive way.

Now, a bit older and a bit wiser, I don't go out looking for opportunities to use tough guy lines and get in trouble as I used to, but I still enjoy watching tough guy movies, both new ones that come out, and revisiting those of yesteryear that I grew up with. That's why working on the *Tough Guy Wisdom* series has been a lot of fun. I watched every movie to collect the quotes and information for this series. I also used on-line and print sources to find the movie and actor trivia that the books contain. The Internet Movie Database, IMDb, provided much assistance in writing these books. I'm grateful to them all.

Some quotes, such as "Opinions vary." (found in this volume) don't seem "tough guy," until you have the setting. That's why I included the setting for each quote included in the *Tough Guy Wisdom* series. You need to picture Morgan (Terry Funk) saying to Dalton (Patrick Swayze), "You know, I heard you had balls big enough to come in a dump truck, but you don't look like much to me." This was Dalton's reply in *Road House* (1989). It's the wise-cracking and coolness in the face of danger or difficult situations that helps endear us to these tough guy heroes.

You will also notice an absence of a few of the most famous of tough guys, specifically John Wayne, Clint Eastwood, Charles Bronson, Arnold Schwarzenegger, Sylvester Stallone, and Chuck Norris. These six Hollywood tough guys will each have their own specific volume in the *Tough Guy Wisdom* series. So, if you are a fan of any, or all, of these actors - stay tuned. Collections of their most famous quotes, movie trivia, and facts about them will be appearing in special volumes to be released later.

I wrote this second volume along with volumes one and three, so if you see a couple of quotes from one of your favorite tough guy movies, but wonder why a specific quote is missing, it may be in one of the others in the series. Or maybe I missed one that you think should be included. If you have a favorite tough guy movie or quote that you believe should be featured, e-mail me at aburrese@aol.com and it will be considered for a future volume.

I sincerely hope that you enjoy reading these tough guy quotes, along with the movie and actor trivia, as much as I enjoyed collecting them. It's pretty cool when you can tell your wife and friends that watching a tough guy movie is actually work. I'm also sure that reading this book will remind you of movies you saw a long time ago and will want to watch again. Take it from me, it is fun to watch them again and remember the first time you saw them, and reminisce a bit. So relax and enjoy a little bit of *Tough Guy Wisdom*.

TOUGH GUY WISDOM II
RETURN OF THE TOUGH GUY

"Just the fly in the ointment, Hans. The monkey in the wrench. The pain in the ass."

Bruce Willis as John McClane – **Die Hard (1988)**

Setting:

McClane's answer to Hans Gruber (Alan Rickman) when asked who he is.

Movie Trivia:

The exterior shots of the Nakatomi building in *Die Hard* (1988) are of the 34 story Fox Plaza in Century City, Los Angeles; the building where author Alain Burrese met President Ronald Reagan, who's office was on the top floor.

About the Actor:

Bruce Willis mainly grew up in Penns Grove, New Jersey.

"Opinions vary."

Patrick Swayze as Dalton – **Road House (1989)**

Setting:

Dalton's reply to Morgan (Terry Funk) on their first meeting when he says, "You know, I heard you had balls big enough to come in a dump truck, but you don't look like much to me."

Movie Trivia:

Road House's Director, Rowdy Harrington, was nominated for a 1990 Razzie Award for Worst Director for *Road House* (1989).

About the Actor:

One of the ways Patrick Swayze paid the bills when he was trying to make it as a dancer or actor was through woodworking and carpentry.

"I already got a guilty conscience. Might as well have the money, too."

Kurt Russell as Wyatt Earp – **Tombstone (1993)**

Setting:

Earp's reply at the beginning of the movie when he refuses to talk to U.S. Marshal Crawley Dake (Gary Clarke as Gary Clark) because he's going to Tombstone to strike it rich, and Dake says, "I'll tell you one thing though, never saw a rich man who didn't wind up with a guilty conscience."

Movie Trivia:

The real Wyatt Earp's fifth cousin, Wyatt Earp, plays Billy Clairborne in the film.

About the Actor:

Kurt Russell's height is reported to be 5'11" (1.80 m).

"This, I'm trained for."

Steven Seagal as Casey Ryback – **Under Siege 2: Dark Territory (1995)**

Setting:

As terrorists take over the train, Ryback dispatches one, and then hides in the freezer when others shoot the cooks. When he comes out of the freezer, he looks at the blood and mess and makes the comment above. This comment is in reference to his earlier comment that he was not trained for dealing with his niece, a teenage girl.

Movie Trivia:

Under Siege 2: Dark Territory (1995) was directed by Geoff Murphy, who also directed another sequel, *Young Guns II* (1990), where he did not direct the first movie.

About the Actor:

Steven Seagal's first wife was Miyako Fujitani. They were married from 1975 to 1986 and have two children, Kentaro Seagal and Ayako Fujitani.

"Well, it doesn't look to me like I really have any choice, now does it?"

Tom Laughlin as Billy Jack – ***Billy Jack (1971)***

Setting:

Billy Jack is confronted in the park by Stuart Posner (Bert Freed) and a group of men. This was Billy's reply to Posner's question, "Really think those Green Beret karate tricks gonna help you against all these boys?"

Movie Trivia:

The fight in the park was actually filmed in two locations due to a halt in filming and relocating. Part of the fight is in Arizona and part is in New Mexico. The Laughlins scouted locations until they found a grey concrete building to match the backdrop in the first half of the scene.

About the Actor:

Tom Laughlin calls his wife, Delores Taylor, Doty, and jokes that it was not her that appeared nude by the river in the film, but a double, who had a larger back end.

"Mark, that's the last thing I want, trouble."

Gregory Peck as Jimmy Ringo – ***The Gunfighter (1950)***

Setting:

Ringo tells his old friend, Mark Strett (Millard Mitchell), who is now the Marshal, that he won't need his deputies, and that he won't be starting anything.

Movie Trivia:

The Gunfighter (1950) was nominated for a 1951 Oscar for Best Writing, Motion Picture Story (William Bowers and Andre De Toth).

About the Actor:

Gregory Peck's height was listed as 6'3" (1.91 m).

"Suck it up. Everybody likes breakfast."

Eric Roberts as Merle "The Butcher" Henche – **The Butcher (2007)**

Setting:

Henche's reply after he beats up two men that approach him at his car before finding out they work for a friend, Larry (Keith David), he owes money to. He says he'll take them all to breakfast and the one holds his stomach where he was kicked and says, "I don't feel like eating breakfast."

Movie Trivia:

Keith David, who plays Larry, has a long list of television and film credits which include: *The Thing* (1982), *Platoon* (1986), *They Live* (1988), *Road House* (1989), *Pitch Black* (2000), *Gamer* (2009), and many more.

About the Actor:

Eric Roberts says he was attracted to play the part of "The Butcher" because of the originality and cleverness of the script. He says it was something he hadn't read or seen before.

"I hurt somebody's feelings once."

Robert De Niro as Sam – ***Ronin (1998)***

Setting:

Sam's reply when Spence (Sean Bean) asks, "You ever kill anybody?"

Movie Trivia:

Sean Bean, who played wannabe Spence, portrayed Boromir in the *Lord of the Rings* trilogy.

About the Actor:

Robert De Niro was born in New York City, New York, USA.

"Sitting in an office, giving other men orders to kill ain't no different than putting a bullet in a man's heart. Let me tell you something. It's the same goddamn thing."

Tom Berenger as Thomas Beckett – ***Sniper (1993)***

Setting:

Becket and Richard Miller (Billy Zane) talk during a break and Miller says, "I'd take a nice office on the Hill over this shit any day." This is Beckett's reply.

Movie Trivia:

Rex Linn, who many recognize as Detective Frank Tripp from *CSI: Miami* (2002 -) can be seen in an uncredited role as a Colonel early in the film.

About the Actor:

Tom Berenger and his third wife, Patricia Alvaran, have one child, a daughter named Scout (born 1988).

"Well, I'd ask them to please go around by the gate."

Alan Ladd as Shane – **Shane (1953)**

Shane's reply, as he's fixing a cut fence, to Joey (Brandon De Wilde), who asks, "Shane, what would you do if you caught them cutting our fence?" Joey is referring to Ryker's (Emilie Meyer) men who the boy told Shane had been cutting other fences.

Movie Trivia:

The June 2008 American Film Institute's list of the 10 greatest films in the "Western" genre rank *Shane* (1953) at number 3.

About the Actor:

Alan Ladd appeared in *Citizen Kane* (1941) as one of the "faceless" reporters who are always shown in silhouette.

"A martial artist has to take responsibility for himself, and to accept the consequences of his own doing."

Bruce Lee as Lee – ***Enter the Dragon (1973)***

Setting:

Lee's reply to the elder Shaolin Temple Abbot (Roy Chiao) when he requests, "Tell me now the Shaolin Commandment Number 13."

Movie Trivia:

Three minutes of footage, not seen in the original U.S. theatrical release, were restored to the Special Edition 25th Anniversary DVD. The philosophical scenes that were cut were important to Lee, who wanted to share his philosophy as well as martial art action.

About the Actor:

Bruce Lee died from a cerebral edema on July 20, 1973, just before the release of his biggest film, *Enter the Dragon* (1973). He left behind his wife, Linda Lee Cadwell, and two children, Brandon Lee and Shannon Lee. He is buried in Lakeview Cemetery, Seattle, Washington.

"I heard God's fast. But I have to go up in front of him myself before I'd bet on him."

Kris Kristofferson as Billy The Kid – **Pat Garrett and Billy the Kid (1973)**

Setting:

After Pat Garrett (James Coburn) and his crew capture Billy The Kid, they are playing a game of cards and Bob Ollinger (R. G. Armstrong) recites scripture and tells Billy, "It's time you got close to God boy." This was Billy's response.

Movie Trivia:

Pat Garrett and Billy the Kid (1973) was directed by Sam Peckinpah. The director is also known for *The Wild Bunch* (1969), *The Killer Elite* (1975), and others.

About the Actor:

Kris Kristofferson earned his jump wings and Ranger tab while serving in the U.S. Army.

"Chief son of a bitch to you."

Tom Selleck as Jesse Stone – **Stone Cold (2005)**

Setting:

Stone's reply, after Stone tells officer Crane (Viola Davis) to take Bo Marino (Shawn Roberts) to the holding cell for the night, and Marino's father, Joe Marino (Thomas Gibson), says to Stone, "You son of a bitch." Stone continues, "Now, unless you want to spend the night here, too, I suggest you and Miss Fiore (Mimi Rogers) go someplace and plan your brutality suit."

Movie Trivia:

Mimi Rogers, who plays Rita Fiore, has appeared in numerous movies and television shows, including *The X-Files* (1998-1999), *Paper Dolls* (1984), and an episode of *Magnum P.I.* (1982) where she played Margo Perina in the series starring Tom Selleck.

About the Actor:

Besides working together on *Magnum P.I.* in 1982, Tom Selleck and Mimi Rogers dated.

"You sure you want to get cute with me?"

Tommy Lee Jones as Chief Deputy Marshal Samuel Gerard – ***U.S. Marshals (1998)***

Setting:

When Special Agent John Royce (Robert Downey, Jr.) is assigned to his team, Gerard asks him, "You have a weapon?" and Royce replies, "Yeah, a big one. How about you?" After the above reply, Royce does show Gerard his weapon, and Gerard tells him to get a back-up weapon and, "Get yourself a Glock. Lose that nickel plated sissy pistol."

Movie Trivia:

Special Agent John Royce's "nickel plated sissy pistol" is a Taurus PT945 .45 caliber handgun.

About the Actor:

After graduating from college, Tommy Lee Jones moved to New York and began his theatrical career on Broadway in *A Patriot for Me.*

"Mama don't like tattletales."

"Rowdy" Roddy Piper as Nada – **They Live (1988)**

Setting:

Said to an alien describing Nada into his wrist watch communication and transportation device. As Nada levels his shotgun toward the alien, he disappears surprising Nada for this is the first time he's seen the "disappearing trick."

Movie Trivia:

The only character in the movie given a first and last name is Holly Thompson (Meg Foster), but you have to listen for it when Nada and Holly are talking in her apartment, because the credits just say, "Holly."

About the Actor:

Roddy Piper and Paul Orndorff lost to Hulk Hogan and Mr. T in the main event of *WrestleMania I* on March 31, 1985, at Madison Square Garden in New York, New York.

"Well, if you're afraid of getting a rotten apple, don't go to the barrel. Get it off the tree."

Sean Connery as Jim Malone – **The Untouchables (1987)**

Setting:

Malone tells Ness (Kevin Costner) that he can trust no one, and Ness then asks where they will get help. This is his answer. The tree in this case is the academy class where they look to draft a new recruit into their small group. They pick up team member Agent George Stone/Giuseppe Petri (Andy Garcia).

Movie Trivia:

Andy Garcia was first asked to read for the part of Frank Nitti, but Garcia convinced them to let him read for the part of George Stone. Billy Drago was then cast as Nitti.

About the Actor:

One of Sean Connery's jobs in Edinburgh was as a lifeguard.

"I'm relaxed! I'm very fuckin' relaxed!"

Samuel L. Jackson as Lt. Danny Roman – **The Negotiator (1998)**

Setting:

Roman schools Farley (Stephen Lee) in the ways of hostage negotiation, especially about never saying 'no' when dealing with a hostage taker, while waiting for Negotiator Sabian (Kevin Spacey) to show up. Farley is in way over his head when trying to talk Roman down.

Movie Trivia:

The Negotiator (1998) was written by James DeMonaco and Kevin Fox.

About the Actor:

Samuel L. Jackson's height is listed as 6'2 ½" (1.89 m).

"You want to apologize to the lady?"

Steve Austin as John Brickner – **Damage (2009)**

Setting:

When a jerk gets friendly with his hands to the bar maid, Frankie (Laura Vandervoot), Brickner steps in and asks if he wants to apologize. He asks as his hands are squeezing the guy's throat. He then escorts the guy out of the bar and is offered a job as the bar's bouncer.

Movie Trivia:

Damage (2009) was written by Frank Hannah. He also wrote *The Cooler* (2003) starring William H. Macy, Alec Baldwin, and Maria Bello.

About the Actor:

Steve Austin was born on December 18, 1964, in Austin, Texas.

"When some wild-eyed, eight-foot tall maniac grabs your neck, taps the back of your favorite head up against the barroom wall, and he looks you crooked in they eye and he asks you if ya paid your dues, well, you just stare that big sucker right back in the eye, and you remember what old Jack Burton always says at a time like that, 'Have ya paid your dues, Jack?' 'Yes sir, the check is in the mail.'"

Kurt Russell as Jack Burton – **Big Trouble in Little China (1986)**

Setting:

Burton driving his truck at the beginning of the movie giving out advice over the CB radio.

Movie Trivia:

Big Trouble in Little China (1986) was originally written as a western set in the 1880s.

About the Actor:

Kurt Russell was the boy Elvis pays a quarter to kick his character Mike Edwards in the shin, so he can go visit nurse Diane Warren (Joan O'Brien) in *It Happened at the World's Fair* (1963).

"So let me go. Just let me go on by, or I'll fuck you up ugly."

Steven Seagal as Shane Daniels – ***A Dangerous Man (2009)***

Setting:

The two thugs outside the liquor store think Daniels is talking shit when he told them he studied how to kill people like them. After he says the above, one thug asks, "What's that mean, 'Fuck you up ugly?'" Daniels replies, "It means your mama won't recognize you in your coffin." The thug pulls a gun and Daniels makes true with his promise.

Movie Trivia:

The tag line for *A Dangerous Man* (2009) is "They Started This. He'll Finish It."

About the Actor:

Steven Seagal released his first music album, "Songs From The Crystal Cave" in 2004.

"I'm surprised you haven't heard about me. You know, I got a bad reputation and sometimes I just go nuts, like now. Don't move. I'll make a deal with you Arjen. Arjen, is that it, or Aryan, or whatever the fuck your name is. I'll make a little deal with you. You fold up your tents, and get the fuck out of my country and I won't do anything to you. I'll leave you alone. Because if you stick around here, I'm gonna fuck your ass. I'm gonna send you home with your balls in a sling, you got that?"

Mel Gibson as Sergeant Martin Riggs – **Lethal Weapon 2 (1989)**

Setting:

Riggs tells Arjen Rudd (Joss Ackland) to leave the country just before shooting Rudd's large fish tank. On the way out of the building, Riggs tells Arjen's assistant, Rika van den Haas (Patsy Kensit), "I've just been upstairs with your boss. You know, shooting the breeze, shooting the fish."

Movie Trivia:

Warren Murphy, author and co-creator/author with Richard Sapir of *The Destroyer* series, worked on the story and shared the credit with Shane Black.

About the Actor:

While reports differ, it is generally accepted that Mel Gibson's height is 5'9" (1.75 m).

"What is this, a tag team?"

Bruce Willis as Lt. John McClane – ***Die Hard 2 Die Harder (1990)***

Setting:

As McClane is fighting one bad guy in the luggage area, another shows up and starts shooting at him. This is McClane talking to himself.

Movie Trivia:

Steven E. de Souza and Doug Richardson wrote the screenplay to *Die Hard 2 Die Harder* (1990).

About the Actor:

After high-school graduation, 18-year-old Willis decided to land a blue-collar job in the vein of his father, and accepted a position at the DuPont Chambers Works factory in Deep Water, NJ, but withdrew after a co-worker was killed on the job.

"My name is Zeus. As in father of Apollo, Mount Olympus? Don't-fuck-with-me-or-I'll-shove-a-lightning-bolt-up-your-ass Zeus! You got a problem with that?"

Samuel L. Jackson as Zeus Carver – **Die Hard With a Vengeance (1995)**

Setting:

Zeus Carver explains to John McClane (Bruce Willis) that his name is Zeus and not Jesus, as they introduce themselves in a cab, just after Zeus saves McClane from a mob who didn't like the derogatory sign he was wearing in the middle of Harlem.

Movie Trivia:

The first part of the movie, including the wearing of the offensive sign and the "My name is Zeus" conversation, is right out of the original *Simon Says* screenplay by Jonathan Hensleigh that was turned into *Die Hard with a Vengeance* (1995).

About the Actor:

Samuel L. Jackson was briefly suspended in 1969 from Morehouse College after taking hostage members of the board of trustees, including the father of the Rev. Dr. Martin Luther King, during a protest of the failure of the university to have black trustees or a black studies program.

"You might not like what you find, Chains."

Brian Bosworth as Joe Huff/John Stone – **Stone Cold (1991)**

Setting:

Stone's reply to gang leader Chains Cooper (Lance Henriksen) when Chains tells him, "It's you and me Stone. We're going to get into each other's heads, man."

Movie Trivia:

Lance Henriksen, the actor who played gang leader Chains, has appeared in a large body of films and television, including Detective Hal Vukivich in *The Terminator* (1984), Bishop in *Aliens* (1986), and as the voice of Kerchak, the Gorilla King, in Disney's *Tarzan* (1999).

About the Actor:

Brian Bosworth signed an $11 million, ten-year, no-cut, all-guaranteed contract to play for the Seattle Seahawks in 1987. At the time, it was the biggest rookie contract in NFL history.

"I shoot them, or Mr. Hitch does."

Ed Harris as Virgil Cole – **Appaloosa (2008)**

Setting:

During Cole's and Randall Bragg's (Jeremy Irons) first meeting in the saloon, Cole tells Bragg that if his boys follow the posted bylaws, everything will be *muy bueno*, but if they don't he'll arrest them. Bragg then asks, "and if they don't go along?" This was Cole's reply.

Movie Trivia:

The first song you hear as the credits role is *Scare Easy*. It was written by Tom Petty and performed by Mudcrutch, Tom Petty's band from 1967 that got back together in 2007, and released a new CD in 2008.

About the Actor:

The second song you hear as the credits roll in *Appaloosa* (2008) is *You'll Never Leave My Heart*. It was written and performed by Ed Harris.

"Goddamn, that hurts, doesn't it?"

Sam Elliott as Wade Garrett – **Road House (1989)**

Setting:

Garrett's comment to the large goon he just dropped with a kick to the knee as he helps Dalton (Patrick Swayze) take on a group of Brad Wesley's (Ben Gazzara) men outside the Double Deuce.

Movie Trivia:

Road House (1989) was released in the U.S. on May 19, 1989. Author, Alain Burrese, was still stationed in South Korea with the U.S. Army at that time, so he was not able to see the movie in the theater. He first saw it when it came on HBO after he returned to the U.S.

About the Actor:

Sam Elliot was nominated for a Golden Globe for Best Performance by an Actor in a Supporting Role in a Series, Mini-Series, or Motion Picture Made for TV for his role as Wild Bill Hickok in *Buffalo Girls* (1995) (TV).

"You want to shit sparks? You just stay put, okay? Stay put."

Forrest Whitaker as Rawlins – **Bloodsport (1988)**

Setting:

Said to Jackson (Donald Gibb), after Jackson tackles both Hemler (Norman Burton) and Rawlins, who are trying to take Frank Dux (Jean Claude Van Damme) back to the U.S. and not let him compete in the Kumite. Jackson's tackle allows Dux to run off. Rawlins holds his taser up for Jackson to see as he says the above, and then goes after Dux.

Movie Trivia:

Both Donald Gibb and Forrest Whitaker appeared in popular comedies of the 80s. Gibb played Fred "The Ogre" Palowakski in *Revenge of the Nerds* (1984), and Whitaker appeared as Charles Jefferson in *Fast Times at Ridgemont High* (1982).

About the Actor:

Forest Whitaker won the 2007 Oscar for Best Performance by an Actor in a Leading Role for his portrayal of Idi Amin in *The Last King of Scotland* (2006).

"You break her heart, I'll break your neck."

Vin Diesel as Dominic Toretto – **The Fast and the Furious (2001)**

Setting:

Toretto discusses dating his sister, Mia (Jordana Brewster), with Brian O'Conner (Paul Walker) as they work on a car.

Movie Trivia:

Writing credits for *The Fast and the Furious* (2001) include: Ken Li (magazine articles "Racer X"), Gary Scott Thompson, Erik Bergquist, and David Ayer.

About the Actor:

Vin Diesel is listed as 6' (1.83 m) tall.

"Don't spend it too soon."

Patrick Swayze as the Nomad – **Steel Dawn (1987)**

Setting:

A bad guy is about to clobber Kasha (Lisa Niemi) with a huge leg of meat, and says, "Damnil's going to pay me more for this." The Nomad steps in and grabs his arm, states the above, and then proceeds to kick butt.

Movie Trivia:

Steel Dawn (1987) is one of the films that Patrick Swayze's real life wife, Lisa Niemi, co-starred with him.

About the Actor:

Patrick Swayze was 19 when he met Lisa Niemi, then 15 years old, when she was attending dance lessons with Patrick Swayze's mom, Patsy Swayze. They married in June, 1975, when Lisa was 19.

"Now I don't want to kill you, and you don't want to be dead."

Danny Glover as Malachi 'Mal' Johnson – **Silverado (1985)**

Setting:

Confronting four men about to kill Mal's friend Emmett (Scott Glenn).

Movie Trivia:

Silverado (1985) was released on July 10, 1985, in the United States.

About the Actor:

Danny Glover married Asake Bomani in 1975.

"Drop it, or die."

Tom Laughlin as Billy Jack – **Billy Jack (1971)**

Setting:

A couple of Posner's (Bert Freed) men go for their rifles when Billy stops them from slaughtering wild horses at the beginning of the movie. Billy fires off two quick shots at men reaching for weapons and then levels his lever action rifle at a man holding a rifle. This is what Billy tells him. Billy then says, "On this reservation, I am the law. So I'll tell you this just once. Have your men drop their guns and you can leave quietly."

Movie Trivia:

Howard Hesseman, who has appeared in numerous roles in television and film, including 90 episodes of *WKRP in Cincinnati* (1978-1982) as Johnny "Dr. Fever" Caravella, appeared as Howard Johnson, the drama teacher, but was credited as Don Sturdy.

About the Actor:

Tom Laughlin directed *Billy Jack* (1971) but used the pseudonym "T.C. Frank" in the credits.

"Never, ever, gamble when you're desperate, Sue."

Eric Roberts as Merle "The Butcher" Henche – ***The Butcher (2007)***

Setting:

Henche's reply when Sue (Garrett Warren) wants him to get out of a car, and tells Henche he brought along his .44 to assist. (That, and a half dozen armed mobsters.) Henche tells him he's too young to make that call, and Sue says, "I guess I'm just going to have to take a gamble at that Butcher Boy." Later, after killing all the mobsters, Henche looks down at Sue's body and says, "Yeah, you should have kept your good eye open, Sue."

Movie Trivia:

Garrett Warren, who played the small role of Sue, was also the 2nd Unit Director and Action Coordinator. Warren has appeared in and done stunt work for many pictures, and he's taught martial arts and fight choreography to many celebrities.

About the Actor:

Eric Roberts earned his second Golden Globe nomination for his portrayal of Paul Snider, the boyfriend and killer of Playmate turned movie star Dorothy Stratten (Played by Mariel Hemingway), in *Star 80* (1983).

"Run." ("No, I mean it, really and truly, what would you do?" – Kinnick) "If he was standing twenty feet away, and ah, I didn't have anything in my hands, I'd be in trouble. But if he got up close to me, got a little Hollywood on me, did like that. I'd stick it up his ass."

Burt Reynolds as Nick 'Mex' Escalante – **Heat (1986)**

Setting:

Escalante's reply when Cyrus Kinnick (Peter MacNicol) asks him what he would do if someone pulled a gun on him.

Movie Trivia:

Peter MacNicol, who played Cyrus Kinnick in *Heat* (1986), played John Cage in 104 episodes of the television series *Ally McBeal* (1997-2002).

About the Actor:

Burt Reynolds says he regrets turning down the role of James Bond when it was offered to him after Sean Connery left. Reynolds said at the time, "An American can't play James Bond."

"Most time, a man will tell you his bad intentions if you listen, let yourself hear. A few years back, a free-graze outfit come through. That weren't no idle story."

Kevin Costner as Charley Waite – ***Open Range (2003)***

Setting:

Waite comments on what he knows is coming when he, Boss Spearman (Robert Duvall), and Button (Diego Luna) discuss the four hooded horsemen watching them. He refers to the earlier conversation he and Boss had with Denton Baxter (Michael Gambon). Baxter told Waite and Spearman about a free-grazing outfit that had a man shot during a cattle stampede in the night.

Movie Trivia:

Charley Waite's dog in the film is named Tig, which is also the name of the film's production company.

About the Actor:

Kevin Costner's grandmother's name was Tig.

"Well, the U.S. government spent a lot of time and money teaching me how not to die after they got done teaching me how to kill people."

Mark Wahlberg as Bob Lee Swagger – **Shooter (2007)**

Setting:

Swagger's reply to Sarah Fenn (Kate Mara) after he tells her he's supposed to be dead, and she asks, "Why aren't you?"

Movie Trivia:

Shooter (2007) was directed by Antoine Fuqua, who also directed *Training Day* (2001) and *Tears of the Sun* (2003), among other films.

About the Actor:

Mark Wahlberg modeled underwear for Calvin Klein in 1992 with supermodel Kate Moss.

"Welcome to America!"

Kurt Russell as Gabe Cash – ***Tango & Cash (1989)***

Setting:

To chase the bad guy who shot him, Cash "borrows" a car from a man who speaks with an accent in the parking garage and proceeds to destroy it. The man catches up and yells, "You crazy guy. What did you do with my car? I believe in Perestroika!" This was Cash's reply.

Movie Trivia:

Tango & Cash (1989) was written by Randy Feldman. Unfortunately, he was nominated for a 1990 Razzie Award for Worst Screenplay.

About the Actor:

Kurt Russell once played a policeman on an episode of *Charlie's Angles* (1978).

"All you have to do is follow three simple rules. One, never underestimate your opponent. Expect the unexpected. Two, take it outside. Never start anything inside the bar unless it's absolutely necessary. And three, be nice."

Patrick Swayze as Dalton – **Road House (1989)**

Setting:

Dalton gives the employees of the Double Deuce three rules during his "speech" to them after being hired to clean the place up.

Movie Trivia:

Producer Joel Silver received a nomination for a 1990 Razzie Award for Worst Picture for *Road House* (1989).

About the Actor:

In the early 1970s, Patrick Swayze sang and played guitar in the clubs down in Greenwich Village.

"This mustn't register on an emotional level. First, distract target. Then block his blind jab. Counter with cross to left cheek. Discombobulate. Dazed, he'll attempt wild haymaker. Employ elbow block, and body shot. Block feral left. Weaken right jaw. Now fracture. Break cracked ribs. Traumatize solar plexus. Dislocate jaw entirely. Heel kick to diaphragm. In summary, ears ringing, jaw fractured, three ribs cracked, four broken, diaphragm hemorrhaging, physical recovery, six weeks, full psychological recovery, six months, capacity to spit at back of head – neutralized."

Robert Downey, Jr. as Sherlock Holmes – **Sherlock Holmes (2009)**

Setting:

Holmes is engaged in a sporting bare knuckle fight in a back alley arena. He tells the man, "That's it, big man, we're done. You won, congratulations." The larger man, McMurdo (David Garrick), says, "We ain't done yet." He then makes a big mistake and spits on the back of Holmes's head. That's when we hear Holmes's thoughts right before making them come true.

Movie Trivia:

Sherlock Holmes (2009) was directed by Guy Ritchie, who also directed *Lock, Stock and Two Smoking Barrels* (1998) and *Snatch* (2000) among others.

About the Actor:

Robert Downey, Jr. was born on April 4, 1965, in Greenwich Village, New York City, NY.

"Snakes. Why did it have to be snakes?"

Harrison Ford as Indiana Jones – **Raiders of the Lost Ark (1981)**

Setting:

Indy's comment as he looks into the Well of Souls. He's not too comforted by Sallah (John Rhys-Davies) saying, "Asps. Very dangerous. You go first."

Movie Trivia:

The hieroglyphics in the Well of Souls include engravings of R2-D2 and C-3PO from *Star Wars* (1977).

About the Actor:

Harrison Ford isn't afraid of snakes one bit, but a sheet of glass still separates him and the cobra when he falls into the Well of Souls.

"Ghettos are the same all over the world. They stink."

Jim Kelly as Williams – ***Enter the Dragon (1973)***

Setting:

Williams and Roper (John Saxon) catch up with each other and look at the Chinese poor from aboard the boat taking the fighters to Han's (Kien Shih) island. Roper replies, "Same old Williams."

Movie Trivia:

Enter the Dragon (1973) was produced by Fred Weintraub and Paul Heller. Fred Weintraub also produced such martial art movies as *Hot Potato* (1976) with Jim Kelly, *Jaguar Lives!* (1979) with Joe Lewis, *The Big Brawl* (1980) with Jackie Chan, *Force Five* (1981) with Joe Lewis and other notable martial artists, *Gymkata* (1985) with Kurt Thomas, and *China O'Brien* (1990) with Cynthia Rothrock.

About the Actor:

James M. Kelly was born in Paris, Kentucky, on May 5, 1946.

"Not me, I'm in my prime."

Val Kilmer as Doc Holliday – **Tombstone (1993)**

Setting:

Holliday's reply to Johnny Ringo (Michael Biehn) when he asks if Holliday is retired too. Holliday then goes on to say, "Ah, you must be Ringo. Look, darlin, Johnny Ringo, the deadliest pistolier since Wild Bill, they say. What do you say, darlin. Should I hate him?" When Kate (Joanna Pacula) says Holliday doesn't even know Ringo, he continues, "No, that's true, but...I don't know, there's just something about him, something around the eyes. I don't know. Reminds me of...me. No, I'm sure of it. I hate him." Next comes the Latin exchange between Holliday and Ringo and the demonstrations with Ringo's pistol and Holliday's cup.

Movie Trivia:

That same year, Joanna Pacula appeared in *Under Investigation* (1993), *Private Lessons II* (1993), *Warlock: The Armageddon* (1993), and *Tombstone* (1993).

About the Actor:

In many of his movies, Val Kilmer twirls small objects with his fingers.

"Only when I have something to say."

Tom Selleck as Jesse Stone – **Stone Cold (2005)**

Setting:

Stone's reply to one of the town counsel members, Jim Burns (John Dunsworth), who are questioning him about his job, when Burns asks, "Damn it, don't you talk?" Another counsel member, Hansen (Jeremy Akerman), tells him how he should do his job, and Stone replies, "I'm a cop. I've been a cop for a long time. I'm good at it. I know how to do this. You don't." Burns tells him, "Damn it, we can fire you." Before getting up and walking out, Stone tells him, "You can. But you can't tell me what to do."

Movie Trivia:

Director Robert Harmon said of *Stone Cold* (2005), "It's classic Robert Parker, a moral man put into an immoral situation, usually a man of few words, that certainly is the case with Jesse Stone."

About the Actor:

Tom Selleck said about the book *Stone Cold*, "I saw a character driven piece with a very flawed guy who was basically a guy who always didn't do everything right, but wanted to do the right thing."

"It's not that I can't fight. I'm not supposed to. It's against my religion, you know? I'm a Buddhist."

Steven Seagal as Lt. Jack Cole – **The Glimmer Man (1996)**

Setting:

Cole and Det. Jim Campbell (Keenen Ivory Wayans) are confronted in a parking garage by Russian mobsters. Before the fight, where Cole takes out a number of them, he tells Campbell that he can't fight. Afterwards, looking at the bodies on the ground, Campbell says, "You know, for a minute there I forgot you said you can't fight." This was Cole's answer.

Movie Trivia:

Kevin Brodbin wrote *The Glimmer Man* (1996).

About the Actor:

Steven Seagal did some slicing and dicing with a credit card in *The Glimmer Man* (1996), but there actually is a Steven Seagal knife that was made by Kershaw Knives. It has his signature in English on one side and in Japanese characters on the other.

"Would you tell me, please, Mr. Howard, why should I trade one tyrant 3,000 miles away for 3,000 tyrants one mile away? An elected legislature can trample a man's rights as easily as a king can."

Mel Gibson as Benjamin Martin – ***The Patriot (2000)***

Setting:

Martin addresses a meeting in regards to South Carolina joining the other colonies to fight the British.

Movie Trivia:

The Patriot (2000) was nominated for three Oscars. The categories were: Best Cinematography, Caleb Deschanel; Best Music, Original Score, John Williams; and Best Sound, Kevin O'Connell, Greg P. Russell, and Lee Orloff.

About the Actor:

Mel Gibson was ranked #12 in *Empire* (UK) magazine's "The Top 100 Movie Stars of All Time" list. October, 1997.

"Tell Mr. Doyle if he'd have hired smarter guys, none of this would have happened."

Bruce Willis as John Smith – ***Last Man Standing (1996)***

Setting:

Smith's comment after filling Finn (Patrick Kilpatrick) full of holes. Finn shouldn't have challenged him.

Movie Trivia:

Last Man Standing (1996) is a retelling of the story in Kurosawa's classic, *Yojimbo* (1961).

About the Actor:

Bruce Willis was paid $16.5 million for his role in *Last Man Standing* (1996).

"Well, Colt makes a heavy firearm. That's a fact."

Ed Harris as Virgil Cole – **Appaloosa (2008)**

Setting:

Cole and Everett Hitch (Viggo Mortensen) go out to see what the men on the ridge overlooking Appaloosa are up to. When his question isn't answered, Cole hits Dean (Luce Rains) in the mouth with his Colt revolver. This was Cole's reply when Dean complains that Cole knocked his tooth out.

Movie Trivia:

Mueller is played by Daniel T. Parker, the son of Robert B. Parker, the author of the novel *Appaloosa*.

About the Actor:

Ed Harris had the novel by Robert B. Parker with him while taking a trip to Ireland with his family and fell in love with the characters and their friendship. He then went forward to make the movie.

"Tell me about an ambush? I ambushed you with a cup of coffee."

Robert De Niro as Sam – **Ronin (1998)**

Setting:

Sam exposes Spence (Sean Bean) as a wannabe when Spence starts to tell the group how to ambush the vehicles for their operation. The breaking point is when he can't tell Sam the color of the boathouse at Hereford where Spence claims to have served with the 22nd Special Air Service.

Movie Trivia:

Sean Bean, who played Spence, starred in *Bravo Two Bravo* (1999), where he plays an S.A.S. sergeant and mentions Hereford as his home base. Hereford was the site of the S.A.S. regimental headquarters, known as Stirling Lines, named after founder Sir David Stirling.

About the Actor:

Robert De Niro's height is listed as 5'9 ½" (1.77 m).

"All right, come on guys. Don't do this. If I don't get breakfast, I get real grumpy. I don't think you'll like me grumpy."

Dolph Lundgren as Sgt. Chris Kenner – **Showdown In Little Tokyo (1991)**

Setting:

Kenner talks to a group of yakuza thugs who wanted "protection" money from the café owner. He takes a knife from one, knocks a gun out of another's hand, and locks a third up while still holding his cup of tea. Police officer Johnny Murata (Brandon Lee) interrupts the fight not knowing Kenner is a fellow police officer.

Movie Trivia:

Showdown in Little Tokyo (1991) was directed by Mark L. Lester, who also directed *Commando* (1995) with tough guy actor Arnold Schwarzenegger.

About the Actor:

Hans Dolph Lundgren was born November 3, 1957, in Stockholm, Sweden.

"Actually, I don't think she gives a shit, she's dead."

Matt Damon as Jason Bourne – **The Bourne Identity (2002)**

Setting:

On the phone, Conklin (Chris Cooper) says to Bourne, "Let's ask Marie what she wants to do." This is Bourne's reply.

Movie Trivia:

Author Robert Ludlum was credited as executive producer for *The Bourne Identity* (2002), and also had the movie in memoriam after he died of a heart attack in March 2001.

About the Actor:

Matt Damon's height is listed as 5' 10" (1.78 m).

"Fuck you and fuck your cause."

Tom Berenger as Thomas Beckett – ***Sniper (1993)***

Setting:

Beckett is tied up and his captor, General Miguel Alavarez (Frederick Miragliotta), looks at his dog tags and states, "We've been looking for you. You've hurt our cause." This was Beckett's response.

Movie Trivia:

Being from Montana, author Alain Burrese always liked the last line of the movie said by Richard Miller (Billy Zane), to Beckett, as they fly away in the helicopter, "There's always Montana."

About the Actor:

Tom Berenger lives in Beaufort, South Carolina, when not working on films.

"Pain don't hurt."

Patrick Swayze as Dalton – **Road House (1989)**

Setting:

Dalton's reply to the Doc, Elizabeth Clay (Kelly Lynch), when she asks, "Do you enjoy pain?" This was after Dalton refuses a local when she prepares to stich up his knife wound.

Movie Trivia:

During *Road House's* (1989) love scene between Patrick Swayze and Kelly Lynch, "These Arms of Mine" by Otis Redding plays on the radio. The same song plays during the love scene with Patrick Swayze and Jennifer Gray in *Dirty Dancing* (1987).

About the Actor:

Patrick Swayze's wife Lisa and his brother Donny Swayze were by his side when he died on September 14, 2009, at his ranch on the outskirts of Los Angeles.

"You're right, but I'll get an 'A' for effort."

Steven Seagal as Nico Toscani – ***Above the Law (1988)***

Setting:

Nico Toscani tells five men who just filled his car with lead to drop their weapons. One steps forward and says, "I don't think you can drop us all, badass." Nico shoots him in the chest and replies with the above quote. The other four obey his next command. (For a moment anyway. Once in the store, Nico's firearm is taken away and he has to dispatch the four with empty hands, destroying the shop in the process.)

Movie Trivia:

Sharon Stone, who was nominated for Best Actress in a Leading role for *Casino* (1995), plays Sara Toscani, Nico's wife.

About the Actor:

Steven F. Seagal was born April 10, 1951, in Lansing, Michigan.

"Do you really wanna jump? Do you wanna? Well, then that's fine with me. Come on! Let's do it, asshole. Let's do it. I want to do it. I want to do it."

Mel Gibson as Sergeant Martin Riggs – **Lethal Weapon (1987)**

Setting:

Martin Riggs to suicidal jumper (Michael Shaner) just before he leaps off the building, with the jumper handcuffed to his arm, into the police air bag below.

Movie Trivia:

Michael Shaner, who played the attempted suicide jumper, McCleary, played Benny in *The Two Jakes* (1990) starring Jack Nicholson.

About the Actor:

Mel Gibson studied acting at the National Institute of Dramatic Art, an Australian national training institute for students of theatre, film, and television.

"Just because I was asleep doesn't mean I couldn't hear you."

Rain as Raizo – ***Ninja Assassin (2009)***

Setting:

Raizo's reply when Mika Coretti (Naomie Harris) is cutting him lose from the stake he's tied to, and he asks, "What took you?" She answers, "You knew I'd come?"

Movie Trivia:

Naomie Harris, who plays Mika in *Ninja Assassin* (2009), has appeared in numerous films and television, including *Pirates of the Caribbean: Dead Man's Chest* (2006) and *Pirates of the Caribbean: At World's End* (2007).

About the Actor:

Rain played Taejo Togokahn in the movie version of *Speed Racer* (2008) with stars that included Susan Sarandon, John Goodman, and Matthew Fox among others.

"You know, it don't matter how we wish things were. It matters how we deal with how they are."

Gary Busey as Buck Matthews – ***Eye of the Tiger (1986)***

Setting:

Matthews interrupts a Bingo game to try and convince the local townspeople to stand up against the crooked sheriff and the gang that has been terrorizing them. It doesn't work and he has to face them alone.

Movie Trivia:

The gang leader, Blade, was played by William Smith, who, like Gary Busey, also appeared in an episode of *Kung Fu* in 1973, and was Clint Eastwood's opponent Jack Wilson in *Any Which Way You Can* (1980).

About the Actor:

Gary Busey was nominated for an Oscar for Best Actor in a Leading Role for *The Buddy Holly Story* (1978).

"Oh, yes I do. Stand up."

Treat Williams as Karl Thomasson – **The Substitute 3: Winner Takes All (1999)**

Setting:

Thomasson's reply to football player Bo Robinson (Ed Cameron) when he asks him to stand, and Bo tells him, "Naw, you don't want none of me, man." Thomasson then gives a lesson to the class regarding defeating superior armies, illustrated with defeating Bo physically as well.

Movie Trivia:

The Substitute 3: Winner Takes All (1999) was shot in sixteen days.

About the Actor:

Treat Williams is a Certified Flight Instructor. He is rated in single and multi-engine airplanes and helicopters. He worked as a professional pilot for a year in the early 1980s.

"It's not your fault Giorgio's a half-wit. You really want to get killed for a half-wit? Let it go. Put it down."

Bruce Willis as John Smith – **Last Man Standing (1996)**

Setting:

After Smith beats up Giorgio Carmonte (Michael Imperioli), he and Giorgio's boss, Fredo Strozzi (Ned Eisenbert), face off pointing handguns at each other.

Movie Trivia:

Bruce Dern plays Sheriff Ed Galt in *Last Man Standing* (1996).

About the Actor:

The first movie appearance of Bruce Willis was in *The First Deadly Sin* (1980). It was an uncredited part as a man entering a diner.

"I should have killed you back in Philly."

Viggo Mortensen as Tom Stall, aka Joey Cusack – **A History of Violence (2005)**

Setting:

After taking out Carl Fogarty's (Ed Harris) men as they confront him in his front yard, Stall is shot in the shoulder by Fogarty. This was his reply when Fogarty points his gun at him and asks, "You got anything to say before I blow your brains out, you miserable prick?" Right before Stall's son, Jack Stall (Ashton Holmes), shoots Fogarty with a shotgun in the back, Fogarty replies, "Yeah Joey, you should have."

Movie Trivia:

A History of Violence (2005) was the last major Hollywood movie to be released in the VHS format.

About the Actor:

Viggo Mortensen's screen debut was as a young Amish Farmer in Peter Weir's *Witness* (1985) starring Harrison Ford.

"When I'm a guest in another man's house, I don't reach into his refrigerator without asking permission."

Dwayne "The Rock" Johnson as Beck – ***The Rundown (2003)***

Setting:

Beck goes to see Hatcher (Christopher Walken) when looking for Travis Walker (Sean William Scott). This was his reply when Hatcher asks him, "Why come to me?"

Movie Trivia:

The leader of the rebels, Manito, was played by martial artist turned actor Ernie Reyes, Jr. He shows off his martial art skills in the dynamic fight scene.

About the Actor:

Dwayne Johnson was nominated for an MTV Movie Award for Best Fight for the fight versus the Kontiki rebels in *The Rundown* (2003).

"Sorry, sir. You can court-martial me if I live, sir."

Steven Seagal as Casey Ryback – **Under Siege (1992)**

Setting:

Ryback's reply to Admiral Bates (Andy Romano) when told, "I see that you completely disobeyed my orders. Correct?" This was right after Tate (Erika Eleniak) told the admiral, "He's in a gunfight right now, I'm gonna have to take a message," before handing Ryback the communication device.

Movie Trivia:

Nine of the actors in *Under Siege* (1992), including Tommy Lee Jones, returned a year later to appear in *The Fugitive* (1993), starring Harrison Ford and also directed by Andrew Davis.

About the Actor:

Steven Seagal created an all-natural 100% juice herbal energy drink called Steven Seagal's Lightening Bolt. It was created in two flavors: Asian Experience and Cherry Charge.

"You don't remember me. We spoke on the phone two days ago. I told you I would find you."

Liam Neeson as Bryan Mills – **Taken (2008, US release 2009)**

Setting:

Mills says this to Marko (Arben Bajraktaraj), the kidnapper who took his daughter, just before he takes out the entire room of thugs.

Movie Trivia:

Taken (2008, US release 2009) was written by Luc Besson and Robert Mark Kamen. The pair also wrote *The Transporter* (2002) starring Jason Statham.

About the Actor:

Liam Neeson was trained by former Special Air Service (SAS) soldier Mick Gould in combatives and weapons handling to prepare him for his role in *Taken* (2008, US release 2009). Gould has worked on numerous movies, including: *Miami Vice* (2006), *Collateral* (2004), *Ronin* (1998), and *The Long Kiss Goodnight* (1996). He is the founder of Nagasu Do Combat Arts Association.

"Don't give me any crap. You owe me big time. If it wasn't for me, you'd be in jail wearing a dress right now."

Michael Pare as Jim Randell – **Merchant of Death (1997)**

Setting:

Over the phone, Randell tells Mac, the Cessna pilot (David Butler), that he needs a lift when he gets to Caracas as well as some hardware.

Movie Trivia:

Merchant of Death (1997) was directed by Yossi Wein, who was the Cinematographer for the Michael Pare film *Point of Impact* (1993).

About the Actor:

Michael Pare has three brothers and six sisters.

"I'm going to enjoy what happens next."

Vin Diesel as Dominic Toretto – **Fast and Furious (2009)**

Setting:

Toretto confronts Fenix Rise (Laz Alonso) about the murder of his girlfriend Letty (Michelle Rodriguez), and he knows the car he rigged to explode is about to go off.

Movie Trivia:

Fast and Furious (2009) was written by Chris Morgan, who also wrote the third installment, *The Fast and the Furious: Tokyo Drift* (2006). *Fast and Furious* (2009) also gave credit to Gary Scott Thompson for the characters.

About the Actor:

Vin Diesel's mother was a psychologist and astrologist.

"Well, let me give you a word of advice. Always bet on black."

Wesley Snipes as John Cutter – **Passenger 57 (1992)**

Setting:

Cutter talks to terrorist Charles Rane (Bruce Payne) on the aircraft phone from the back of the plane and asks, "Charlie, you ever play roulette?" This was Cutter's reply when Rane answers, "On occasion."

Movie Trivia:

Writing credits for *Passenger 57* (1992) go to Stewart Raffill, Dan Gordon, and David Loughery. Dan Gordon was also one of the writers for *Wyatt Earp* (1994) starring Kevin Costner.

About the Actor:

Wesley Snipes' first movie role was in the football comedy *Wildcats* (1986) starring Goldie Hawn. Snipes played the character Trumaine.

"You think that's good, you should see me spell my name in the snow."

Clive Owen as Smith – ***Shoot 'Em Up (2007)***

Setting:

Smith's reply to Hertz (Paul Giamatti) when he asked who trained him, and says whoever it was, he hadn't lost his aim.

Movie Trivia:

It is reported that they used 15 gallons of fake blood filming *Shoot 'Em Up* (2007), and that the body count for the flim is 106.

About the Actor:

Clive Owen made his film debut in the British-made *Vroom* (1988) co-starring with David Thewlis.

"This is my kind of game, Joe."

Alan Ladd as Shane – **Shane (1953)**

Setting:

Joe Starrett (Van Heflin) is preparing to go face Rufus Ryker (Emile Meyer) and Jack Wilson (Jack Palance) when Shane comes in with his gun on. Joe tells him it ain't his game, and Shane tells him, "Maybe you're a match for Ryker, maybe not. But you're not a match for Wilson." When Shane tells Joe it's no use, and Joe asks if he'll have to fight Shane too, Shane tells him, "That depends on you." The two fight and Shane knocks Joe out with his gun and rides off to town to face Ryker and Wilson.

Movie Trivia:

Van Heflin, who played Joe Starrett, appeared in numerous movies, including *3:10 to Yuma* (1957), *Stagecoach* (1966), and *Airport* (1970).

About the Actor:

Alan Ladd was married to Sue Carol from 1942 through the time of his death in 1964. They had two children, Alana Ladd and David Ladd.

"You come up here, old buddy."

Joe Lewis as Jonathan Cross (Jaguar) – ***Jaguar Lives! (1979)***

Setting:

Cross yells down to his former partner, Bret Barrett (Anthony De Longis), to come to the roof where they have their final fight.

Movie Trivia:

Jaguar Lives! (1979) was directed by Ernest Pintoff, who directed many television series episodes, including *The Six Million Dollar Man* (1975), *The Bionic Woman* (1978), *Kojak* (1975-1978), *Hawaii Five-O* (1976-1978), *The White Shadow* (1979), *Dukes of Hazzard* (1979), *MacGyver* (1985), and many more.

About the Actor:

Joe Lewis has been voted the greatest fighter in karate history. He is one of very few who defeated action star Chuck Norris when Norris was competing.

"I think there was a reason."

Tom Selleck as Jesse Stone – **Stone Cold (2005)**

Setting:

Inside Stone's office, Bo Marino (Shawn Roberts) calls Candace Pennington (Alexis Dziena), the girl he and two others raped, a "little bitch." Her father, Chuck Pennington (Ralph Small), also in the room, stands and punches Bo in the mouth. Bo's father, Joe (Tony De Santis) jumps into the fight and Mr. Pennington lays them both out. The fight broke up, Joe yells he wants Pennington arrested for assault. Stone, who watched the entire episode, shielding Candice from the men, walks over and tells Mr. Pennington, "Sit down, Mr. Pennington. I promise they won't assault you again." He goes on to tell what he saw to Joe, "I saw you and Bo insult Candice Pennington and attack her father." This was Stone's response when Joe says, "He punched my kid for no reason."

Movie Trivia:

Shawn Roberts, who plays Bo Marino, appears as David Burnham in *Edge of Darkness* (2010) starring Mel Gibson.

About the Actor:

Tom Selleck said the scene where Mr. Pennington gets a little justice is a very satisfying scene for an audience.

"No. I only do needlepoint."

Bruce Willis as Lt. John McClane – **Die Hard 2 Die Harder (1990)**

Setting:

Reporter Samantha 'Sam' Coleman (Sheila McCarthy) recognizes McClane from the Nakatomi incident in L.A., and tries to get the scoop from him. She says, "Give me a break. I saw the stiff. Word is that was your handiwork." This is McClane's answer.

Movie Trivia:

Sheila McCarthy, who plays Sam Coleman, has a long list of movie and television roles, including: Laura Murray in *Emily of New Moon* (1998-2002), and Sarah Hamoudi in *Little Mosque on the Prairie* (2007-2009).

About the Actor:

Bruce Willis is a supporter of the Republican party.

"Sorry!"

John Cena as Det. Danny Fisher – ***12 Rounds (2009)***

Setting:

Fisher takes a fire truck to race across town to complete one of Miles Jackson's (Aidan Gillen) 12 near-impossible tasks. As he smashes through anything and everything in his way, he yells back to a man after completely demolishing the man's white car.

Movie Trivia:

John Cena did most of the stunt driving himself with the cars, but when it came to the fire truck, Mike Ryan, a fire truck stunt driver, was controlling the large truck with a steering wheel on the right side of the truck, while the steering wheel Cena used on camera was only for show.

About the Actor:

John Cena trained with the New Orleans Police Department in order to do his own stunt driving for the car chase scenes in *12 Rounds* (2009). Cena said the training was a lot of fun.

"It's just been revoked."

Danny Glover as Roger Murtaugh – ***Lethal Weapon 2 (1989)***

Setting:

After shooting Riggs, Arjen Rudd (Joss Ackland) holds up his identification and claims, "Diplomatic immunity!" Murtaugh shoots him in the forehead and says the above. He then tells Riggs, "They've been de-kaffirnated."

Movie Trivia:

Riggs pushes Murtaugh out of the cargo container just as he starts to say his classic line, "I'm too old for this…"

About the Actor:

Danny Glover's character, in a 2009 episode of *My Name Is Earl* (2009), spoofs his most famous line from the *Lethal Weapon* series by saying, "I'm getting too old for this crap."

"Do it while you're running."

Steven Seagal as Shane Daniels – **A Dangerous Man (2009)**

Setting:

Daniels' reply to Tia (Marlaina Mah) when she sees bloody bodies outside the hotel room after the two are attacked in their room and have to leave quickly. She says, "Oh, God. I think I'm going to be sick."

Movie Trivia:

Marlaina Mah, who played Tia, only has one other big screen credit, and that was as a Lusting Model in *Fantastic Four* (2005).

About the Actor:

Steven Seagal and Kelly LeBrock, his second wife, had three children before their 1996 divorce: Annaliza, Dominich, and Arissa.

"I'm going to give you assholes a chance. What do you say we play a little Bangkok rules? Nobody draws until this hits the ground. You ready? (throws can, draws and shoots, can hits ground) Draw."

Kurt Russell as Snake Plissken – ***Escape from L.A. (1996)***

Setting:

Snake squares off against four men ready to take him in. He teaches them Bangkok rules and kills all four while the can is in the air.

Movie Trivia:

Jeff Imada, who played Saigon Shadow, also appeared in John Carpenter's *They Live* (1988) and *Big Trouble in Little China* (1986). The latter also starred Kurt Russell.

About the Actor:

Kurt Russell reportedly practiced playing basketball between scenes so he could make his own shots in the basketball scene for *Escape From L.A.* (1996).

"You're too stupid to have a good time."

Patrick Swayze as Dalton – ***Road House (1989)***

Setting:

Dalton stops a guy with a blade in his boot from coming into the Double Deuce by saying they are closed. When the guy asks what all the people are doing, Dalton tells him drinking and having a good time. He says that's why he's there as he throws a kick at Dalton. Dalton grabs the kick, says the line above, and begins to kick butt.

Movie Trivia:

Writing credits for *Road House* (1989) go to David Lee Henry (story and screenplay) and Hilary Henkin (screenplay).

About the Actor:

In 1971, Patrick Swayze started San Jacinto Junior College on a gymnastics scholarship with dreams of making the Olympic gymnastics team. The knee injury from his high school football days kept him from realizing that dream.

"And I get to live with myself 24 hours a day."

Bruce Willis as Joe Hallenback – **The Last Boy Scout (1991)**

Setting:

Hallenbeck's reply to his wife Sarah (Chelsea Field) when she says, "I'm not the one who hates you, Joe. You're the one who hates you."

Movie Trivia:

The $1.75 million Shane Black received for his screenplay was the highest paid for a script up to 1990.

About the Actor:

Willis said about the character Hallenbeck, "You have to find the subtle details in his personality that emerge from the stereotype of failure. Then the audience can root for him."

"Read him his rights even though he's a little unconscious."

Steven Seagal as Lt. Jack Cole – **The Glimmer Man (1996)**

Setting:

Cole and Det. Jim Campbell (Keenen Ivory Wayans) question one of the Russian mafia after the fight in the parking garage. After Campbell beats the mobsters head against the hood of the car demanding answers, Cole tells him, "You speak good Russian," to which Campbell replies, "Yes, Black Russian." After the quote above, Campbell too tired to mess with Miranda says, "He knows them."

Movie Trivia:

The Glimmer Man (1996) was one of several Steven Seagal movies, and many, many tough guy movies, that Jeff Imada did stunts for.

About the Actor:

Steven Seagal worked as the martial arts coordinator for the film *The Challenge* (1982) starring Scott Glenn.

"I'm a little careful with everyone."

Tom Selleck as Jesse Stone – **Stone Cold (2005)**

Setting:

Talking while looking at the ocean, Stone tells Captain Healy (Stephen McHattie) he knows who the two killers are, and that they have an interest in him. Healy, talking about the killers, tells Stone, "Jesse, you might want to be a little careful with these people." This was Stone's reply.

Movie Trivia:

The character Captain Healy was played by Scott Wickware in *Spencer: Small Vices* (1999), another movie based on a series by Robert B. Parker.

About the Actor:

Tom Selleck vocally supported President Ronald Reagan throughout the 1980s.

"Well, that's good news. Snakes on crack."

Samuel L. Jackson as Neville Flynn – ***Snakes on a Plane (2006)***

Setting:

Agent Flynn's response when Dr. Steven Price (Todd Louiso) informs him that there must be some kind of pheromone provoking hyper-aggression, like some kind of drug.

Movie Trivia:

Todd Louiso, who played Dr. Steven Price, played Chad the Nanny in *Jerry Maguire* (1996).

About the Actor:

Samuel Jackson had a small role as Stacks Edwards in *Goodfellas* (1990) starring Robert De Niro. De Niro played a supporting role in *Jackie Brown* (1997) where Pam Grier and Samuel Jackson had top billing.

"Intellectually, philosophically. The nuts are good."

Burt Reynolds as Nick 'Mex' Escalante – **Heat (1986)**

Setting:

Escalante's reply to Cyrus Kinneck's (Peter MacNicol) question, "When you have determined there is going to be violence. Where do you like to strike? Intellectually or philosophically speaking."

Movie Trivia:

Nick Escalante's business partner, Pinchus Zion, was played by Howard Hesseman, also known as Johnny 'Dr. Fever' Caravella in the hit television comedy *WKRP in Cincinnati* (1978 – 1982).

About the Actor:

Burt Reynolds played Quint Asper in 50 episodes of *Gunsmoke* (1955 – 1975) in the 1960s.

"You want to plan your moves. Pick your place to fight. Don't make any threats. And don't you ever walk away from one you hear? Good bye, Max."

Brian Keith as Jonas Cord – **Nevada Smith (1966)**

Setting:

Cord shares some parting wisdom with Max Sand, aka Nevada Smith (Steve McQueen), after teaching him how to use a gun and other life skills.

Movie Trivia:

The slogan on one movie poster for *Nevada Smith* (1966) read, "Now a name…soon a legend."

About the Actor:

Brian Keith is one of many actors, including John Wayne, Billy Bob Thornton, and Fess Parker, to play Col. Davy Crockett.

"That's right. And I'm gonna kill every son of a bitch that comes to take them."

Robert Duval as Boss Spearman – ***Open Range (2003)***

Setting:

Spearman's reply to Charley Waite (Kevin Costner) when Waite asks if Spearman is just going to sit out waiting with the cows, after Spearman instructs Waite to take Button (Diego Luna), who is shot, to the doctor in town.

Movie Trivia:

Open Range (2003) was based on the novel *The Open Range Men* by Lauran Paine, who's 1957 novel *Law Man* was made into the movie *The Quiet Gun* (1957) starring Forrest Tucker.

About the Actor:

Robert Duval's motion picture debut was as Boo Radley in *To Kill a Mockingbird* (1962).

"I'll get better. Then I'm going to burn their playhouse down."

Mark Wahlberg as Bob Lee Swagger – **Shooter (2007)**

Setting:

While lying in bed, Swagger learns from Sarah Fenn (Kate Mara) that the reports say he shot his own dog because he knew he wasn't coming back. Then he answers her question, "What are you gonna do?"

Movie Trivia:

Kate Mara, who plays Sarah Fenn, appears as Bethany Cabe in *Iron Man 2* (2010).

About the Actor:

Mark Wahlberg served 50 days in prison at Deer Island penitentiary for assault. He credits his jail time as his motivation to improve his lifestyle and leave crime behind him.

"You bite me, chief, we ain't gonna be friends after."

Steve Austin as John Brickner – **Damage (2009)**

Setting:

Brickner's comment to his first opponent in an underground fight. The guy's teeth were sharpened, and Frankie (Laura Vandervoort) told Brickner, "he bites." After winning the fight, Brickner says, "I can't believe that son of a bitch bit me."

Movie Trivia:

Laura Vandervoort, who plays Frankie, appeared as Kara in 21 episodes of *Smallville* (2007-2008).

About the Actor:

Steve Austin's mom's name is Beverly, and in his book, *The Stone Cold Truth,* he says, "I love and respect her more than any other person in this world. I'll help you read between the lines. *Don't mess with Stone Cold's mom!"*

"Trust me Jackie, I do this for a living."

Eric Roberts as Merle "The Butcher" Henche – **The Butcher (2007)**

Setting:

Henche and Jackie (Irina Bjorklund) are hiding behind the wheel of a vehicle as mobsters shoot at them. The line above is just after Henche tells her, "It's loud and it's scary, but it's harmless, okay. These guys can't shoot. Now, when I shoot back, they're going to duck. When they duck, we go. We can do this. You can do this."

Movie Trivia:

Irina Bjorklund, who plays Jackie, was born in Sweden and is one of the most popular Finnish film stars of the late 90s and early 2000s.

About the Actor:

Eric Roberts once played the newspaper boy in a production of *A Streetcar Named Desire* starring Shirley Knight and Glenn Close.

"Life is a chess game, Juan. This is a crucial move. I want you to think it over."

Tom Berenger as Jonathan Shale – **The Substitute (1996)**

Setting:

Juan Lacas (Marc Anthony) is late for class and Shale tells him he will write "I'm sorry" on the blackboard 100 times. They have a stand-off to see if Juan will do it. This was Shale's advice.

Movie Trivia:

Marc Anthony, who played gang leader Juan Lacas, won an ALMA award for Outstanding Performance of a Song for a Feature Film for the song "I Want To Spend My Lifetime Loving You" in *The Mask of Zorro* (1998).

About the Actor:

Tom Berenger's debut film role was as Richard Moore in *Rush It* (1976).

"You carry a badge? Carry a gun."

Sean Connery as Jim Malone – **The Untouchables (1987)**

Setting:

Malone tells Ness (Kevin Costner) and Stone (Andy Garcia) they are going on a liquor raid and they need another man. Accountant/Agent Oscar Wallace (Charles Martin Smith) comes in and Malone hands him a gun, and tells him the above. The four then go on the raid at the U.S. Post Office building.

Movie Trivia:

Director Brian De Palma states in an interview that Charles Martin Smith has a lot of nebbish charm to him, and that the actor was on the list right from the beginning.

About the Actor:

After three years of naval service, a long bout with a stomach ulcer shortened Sean Connery's naval career.

"I'm givin' you a choice. Either put on these glasses or start eatin' that trash can."

"Rowdy" Roddy Piper as Nada – **They Live (1988)**

Setting:

Nada tries to get Frank (Keith David) to try on the glasses that reveal the aliens and the subliminal messages. Frank replies, "Not this year," and the fight is on.

Movie Trivia:

The fight between Nada (Piper) and Frank (David) was supposed to be a twenty second fight. However, after Piper and David rehearsed and fought it out for real, except for face and groin hits, Carpenter decided to keep the five minute and twenty second scene intact.

About the Actor:

The official website of Hot Rod Rowdy Piper is www.rowdyroddypiper.com.

Alain Burrese

"We don't. I do."

Tommy Lee Jones as Chief Deputy Marshal Samuel Gerard – ***U.S. Marshals (1998)***

Setting:

Gerard and Special Agent John Royce (Robert Downey, Jr.) are on a plane discussing Gerard's getting shot in the swamp. Royce says, "I thought we don't take our work personally." This was Gerard's reply.

Movie Trivia:

Robert Downey, Jr. played Special Agent John Royce, who turned out to be a bad guy in *U.S. Marshals* (1998). Ten years later, he starred as the superhero Tony Stark in the hit *Iron Man* (2008), and then its sequels.

About the Actor:

Tommy Lee Jones was born September 15, 1946, in San Saba, Texas.

"Bernard, I wish you would. I really wish you would."

Tom Laughlin as Billy Jack – **Billy Jack (1971)**

Setting:

After Billy gives Bernard Posner (David Roya) a choice between driving his car into the lake or getting a dislocated elbow, Bernard asks, "What if I drive away? Or take the knife?" After Billy's response, Jean (Delores Taylor) tells Bernard he doesn't have a chance and he chooses to drive the car into the lake.

Movie Trivia:

According to *The Untold Story Behind The Legend of Billy Jack* by Jorge Casuso, the movie cost $300,000 to make and raked in more than $80 million in 1970s dollars. Some of the budget was for the Corvette Bernard drives into the lake.

About the Actor:

Tom Laughlin and Delores Taylor signed author Alain Burrese's copy of *The Untold Story Behind The Legend of Billy Jack* by Jorge Casuso.

"Then we're both fucked."

Bruce Willis as John McClane – **Die Hard With a Vengeance (1995)**

Setting:

McClane gets out of the cab to get on the train and discover the bomb. He tells Zeus Carver (Samuel L. Jackson) to continue to the phone for Simon's (Jeremy Irons) call. He says, "Listen, you fail, I cover your ass. I fail, you cover my ass." This was his response when Carver then asks, "and if we both fail?"

Movie Trivia:

John McTiernan, who directed the first *Die Hard* (1988), was back to direct the third installment: *Die Hard With a Vengeance* (1995).

About the Actor:

Bruce Willis lost his brother, Robert, to pancreatic cancer in 2001. Robert was 42 years old.

"This whole thing fucking sucks!"

Kurt Russell as Gabe Cash – **Tango & Cash (1989)**

Setting:

After Tango (Sylvester Stallone) makes an eloquent speech stating he hopes the trial doesn't tarnish the reputation of the police force, Cash stands to take a turn. He's not as eloquent or forgiving as Tango. His statement causes the police in attendance to cheer.

Movie Trivia:

Tango's sister, and Cash's love interest, Katherine 'Kiki' Tango, is played by Teri Hatcher, who went on to star in the television hits *Lois & Clark: The New Adventures of Superman* (1993 – 1997) and *Desperate Housewives* (2004 – 2012) among many other roles.

About the Actor:

Kurt Russell reportedly auditioned for the role of Han Solo in *Star Wars: Episode IV – A New Hope* (1977).

"Before you learn to fight, you must first learn to meditate."

Patrick Swayze as the Nomad – **Steel Dawn (1987)**

Setting:

Nomad starts teaching the young boy, Jux (Bret Hool), after making him promise he'll never misuse the knowledge if he teaches him the secret of being a good fighter.

Movie Trivia:

Brett Hool, who played the boy Jux, is the son of *Steel Dawn's* (1987) director Lance Hool.

About the Actor:

Patrick Swayze played Danny Zuko in the original Broadway production of *Grease*.

"We are doing something. We're sitting here, waiting."

Robert De Niro as Sam – **Ronin (1998)**

Setting:

Sam's reply to Gregor (Stellan Skarsgard) when he states, "It would be nice to do something." The group is waiting in the apartment until the designated time to go do the job.

Movie Trivia:

Stellan Skarsgard, who played Gregor, also played Bootstrap Bill Turner in *Pirates of the Caribbean: Dead Man's Chest* (2006) and *Pirates of the Caribbean: At World's End* (2007).

About the Actor:

Robert De Niro had a long time relationship with African-American fashion model Toukie Smith.

"Sorry, boss, but there's only two men I trust. One of them's me. The other's not you."

Nicolas Cage as Cameron Poe – ***Con Air (1997)***

Setting:

Poe's response to U.S. Marshal Vince Larken (John Cusack) the first time they meet at the airfield and are pointing guns at each other. Larken asks Poe if he's gonna lower his gun if he lowers his.

Movie Trivia:

Con Air (1997) was nominated for two Oscars. One for Best Music, Original Song for the song "How Do I Live" (Diane Warren), and the other for Best Sound (Kevin O'Connell, Greg P. Russell, Art Rochester).

About the Actor:

In 1983, Nicolas Cage landed roles in his uncle's film *Rumble Fish* (1983) and *Valley Girl* (1983). *Valley Girl* (1983) was released first and launched his career.

"Boards don't hit back."

Bruce Lee as Lee – **Enter the Dragon (1973)**

Setting:

Before their match, Oharra (Bob Wall) breaks a board with a punch to try and impress and intimidate Lee. It doesn't do either. In the famous cinema battle, Lee not only embarrasses and defeats Oharra, but kills him and revenges his sister.

Movie Trivia:

Robert "Bob" Wall appeared with Bruce Lee in three of his movies. These included *Way of the Dragon* (1972), that also featured Chuck Norris; *Enter the Dragon* (1973); and *Game of Death* (1979), the movie that was incomplete when Bruce Lee died. Rumors surround the fight between Lee and Wall in *Enter the Dragon* (1973), but Lee and Wall were actually good friends.

About the Actor:

Bruce Lee staged the fight sequences for *Enter the Dragon* (1973) and received screen credit at the beginning of the movie for this role.

Alain Burrese

"You're dealing with me Ryker."

Alan Ladd as Shane – **Shane (1953)**

Setting:

Shane goes into the bar near the end of the movie and asks Ryker (Emile Meyer) for his offer. Ryker tells Shane, "I'm not dealing with you. Where's Starrett?" Shane tells him the above, and as they talk, he tells Ryker, "You've lived too long. Your kind of days are over." Ryker replies, "My days? What about yours, gunfighter?" Shane answers, "The difference is, I know it."

Movie Trivia:

Writing credits for *Shane* (1953) go to: A.B. Guthrie, Jr. (screenplay); Jack Sher (additional dialogue); and Jack Schaefer (novel).

About the Actor:

Alan Ladd played Nevada Smith in *The Carpetbaggers* (1964), and was interested in the movie that Steve McQueen went on to star in: *Nevada Smith* (1966).

"Hey man, let me give you a hand."

Wesley Snipes as John Cutter – **Passenger 57 (1992)**

Setting:

Cutter finds the handcuffed terrorist conscious, and punches him to knock him cold again, saying the above.

Movie Trivia:

Passenger 57 (1992) was directed by Kevin Hooks, who also directed *Black Dog* (1998) with tough guy Patrick Swayze.

About the Actor:

Wesley Snipes appeared in Michael Jackson's *Bad* (1987) music video.

"I don't remember. That's the second thing they teach you."

Robert De Niro as Sam – ***Ronin (1998)***

Setting:

Sitting in a car, Vincent (Jean Reno) asks, "Under the bridge, by the river, how did you know it was an ambush?" Sam replies, "Whenever there is any doubt, there is no doubt. That's the first thing they teach you." Vincent then asks, "Who taught you?" This was Sam's answer.

Movie Trivia:

The figure skater, Natacha Kirilova, is announced as having won two Olympic and three World Championships. Kirilova was played by Katarina Witt, winner of two Olympic Gold medals (1984 Sarajevo Olympics and 1988 Calgary Olympics), and four World Championships (1984, 1985, 1987, and 1988) in figure skating.

About the Actor:

Robert De Niro formed his own production company, TriBeCa Productions, in 1989.

"I don't box, I fight."

Tom Selleck as Jesse Stone – **Stone Cold (2005)**

Setting:

Stone talks to Candace (Alexis Dziena) about how things are going. She was proud of her father fighting for her, and tells Stone he boxed, and Stone tells her he must have been good. Then she asks Stone, "Did you ever box?" After his answer, she asks, "What's the difference?" Stone replies, "Rules."

Movie Trivia:

Alexis Dziena, who plays Candace, appeared in 21 episodes of *Invasion* (2005 – 2006) as Kira Underlay.

About the Actor:

Tom Selleck maintains a summer home in Jonesboro, Maine.

"Listen, I only shot you in one foot.   Hobble to a hospital."

*Steven Seagal as Lt. Jack Cole – **The Glimmer Man (1996)***

Setting:

Cole interrogates Mr. Smith (Brian Cox) by shooting him in a foot, and then a hand, before Smith tells him what he needs to know.   Cole then leaves Smith by the side of the road, and tells him the above when Smith asks for an ambulance.

Movie Trivia:

Brian Cox, who played Mr. Smith in *The Glimmer Man* (1996), can also be seen as Ward Abbott in the *Bourne* movies.

About the Actor:

In 2004, Steven Seagal appeared in a Mountain Dew commercial.

"And when a man sticks a gun in your face, you got two choices. You can die, or you can kill the motherfucker."

Sam Elliott as Wade Garrett – **Road House (1989)**

Setting:

Garrett and Dalton (Patrick Swayze) discuss old times that haunt Dalton, while waiting for Elizabeth Clay (Kelly Lynch) to return from the ladies room.

Movie Trivia:

Swayze says the exhaustion you see on his face when fighting ex-Navy SEAL turned actor, Marshall Teague, who played Jimmy, was legit. They put contact into the fight to make it look real.

About the Actor:

Sam Elliott's future wife, Katharine Ross, co-starred in *Butch Cassidy and the Sundance Kid* (1969), Elliot's debut film. However, the two did not meet until they filmed *The Legacy* (1978) together.

"Sure, here's my warrant. (strikes man in groin with butt of gun) How do you think he feels now? Better...or worse?"

Sean Connery as Jim Malone – **The Untouchables (1987)**

Setting:

Malone is telling everyone in the stock room of the Post Office building with crates of alcohol they are under arrest. When one man gets in his face and asks if he has a warrant, the above is Malone's reply with a strike to the groin with the butt of his gun.

Movie Trivia:

The Untouchables (1987) won a Grammy for Best Album of Original Instrumental Background Score Written for a Motion Picture or Television. The original score was written by Ennio Morricone and was also nominated for an Oscar.

About the Actor:

Sean Connery won the Golden Globe award for Best Performance by an Actor in a Supporting Role in a Motion Picture for his performance as Jimmy Malone in *The Untouchables* (1987).

"I like ice. Leave it the fuck alone."

Bruce Willis as Joe Hallenbeck – **The Last Boy Scout (1991)**

Setting:

Hallenbeck's reply to Jimmy Dix (Damon Wayans) when he tries to start up a conversation and says, "I'm just trying to break the ice."

Movie Trivia:

To prepare for his role as an athlete, Wayons shaved his head and spent six months working out with a trainer. He went from 169 pounds to 204. He then got down to 194 at the beginning of the film and was 174 on the last day. Wayons said, "In some of the scenes I'm really huge. And in others I look like a bald-headed Michael Jackson."

About the Actor:

Bruce Willis earned an Emmy in 2000 for Outstanding Guest Actor in a Comedy Series for his work on *Friends* (2000).

"Look, you shouldn't go around hurting people. (And why is that?) Because they might just hurt you back."

Phillip Rhee as Tommy Lee – **Best of the Best 4: Without Warning (1998)**

Setting:

When Tommy Lee is escaping from where the bad guys had him tied up, he enters a room full of men training with escrima sticks. The above was the short conversation with the leader of the group before the big fight that included sticks and fencing.

Movie Trivia:

Simon Rhee, Phillip Rhee's brother, who stared as Dae Han in the first two *Best of the Best* films, was stunt coordinator of this film as he was for *Best of the Best 3: No Turning Back* (1995). Hapkido instructor Fariborz Azhakh is listed in the credits as one of the "martial artists."

About the Actor:

Phillip Rhee wrote, directed, and acted as executive producer of *Best of the Best 4: Without Warning* (1998).

"Then Virgil and I can come into that cell and beat the sweet Jesus hell out of you every morning for breakfast if we want to."

Viggo Mortensen as Everett Hitch – **Appaloosa (2008)**

Setting:

As they wait in the jail, this is Hitch's reply to prisoner Randall Bragg (Jeremy Irons) who, after being told to stay quiet, says, "I can speak if I want to."

Movie Trivia:

Ariadna Gil plays Katie, Everett Hitch's love interest in *Appaloosa* (2008).

About the Actor:

Viggo Mortensen played Diego Alatriste in the movie *Alatriste* (2006). This movie also featured Ariadna Gil as Maria de Castro.

"Travis, there is no option 'C.'"

Dwayne "The Rock" Johnson as Beck – **The Rundown (2003)**

Setting:

Beck finds Travis Walker (Seann William Scott) and gives him two options, "A" the easy way to go back to L.A. with him, or "B" which he didn't recommend. Travis then says he'll take option "C." This is Beck's answer.

Movie Trivia:

Seann William Scott played the popular character Steve Stifler in the first three *American Pie* movies.

About the Actor:

Dwayne Douglas Johnson was born May 2, 1972, in Hayward, California.

"What do you know, we had a little falling out."

Michael Pare as Jim Randell – **Merchant of Death (1997)**

Setting:

Randell's reply to Mac, the Cessna pilot (David Butler), when asked, "Where's your passenger?" The passenger was Velazquez (Tony Caprari), who plunged to his death over a cliff after a fight with Randell. Suiting finish since he was the person who killed Randell's family when Randell was a kid, including throwing Randell's father from a cliff.

Movie Trivia:

Merchant of Death (1997) was written by Danny Lerner and David Sparling. Lerner was also a producer for *Merchant of Death* (1997), as well as a producer for *The Order* (2001) starring Jean-Claude Van Damme and also featuring Charlton Heston.

About the Actor:

Michael Pare was born on October 9, 1959, in Brooklyn New York.

"I don't make things complicated, that's just the way things get all by themselves."

Mel Gibson as Sergeant Martin Riggs – **Lethal Weapon (1987)**

Setting:

Riggs and Murtaugh (Danny Glover) discuss the murder of Amanda Hunsaker (Jackie Swanson) while having a beer on Murtaugh's boat after dinner.

Movie Trivia:

Jackie Swanson, who played Amanda Hunsacker, also played Kelly Gaines Boyd in 24 episodes of the popular television show *Cheers* (1989-1993). Kelly joined the show as Woody Boyd's (Woody Harrelson) love interest.

About the Actor:

Mel Gibson was chosen as *People* magazine's first "Sexiest Man Alive" in 1985.

"Believe me, boy, you don't ever want to know. Not ever."

Kurt Russell as Wyatt Earp – **Tombstone (1993)**

Setting:

When Earp learns that brothers Virgil Earp (Sam Elliott) and Morgan Earp (Bill Paxton) have become lawmen in Tombstone, he tells brother Morgan about taking a man's life and how Morgan does not know how that feels.

Movie Trivia:

Tombstone's (1993) director, George P. Cosmatos, also directed *Rambo: First Blood Part II* (1985) and *Cobra* (1986), both starring Sylvester Stallone.

About the Actor:

In 1960, Walt Disney himself signed Russell to a 10-year contract.

"There's no amount of money."

Patrick Swayze as Dalton – **Road House (1989)**

Setting:

Dalton's reply to Brad Wesley (Ben Gazzara) when he invited Dalton to his place and asks, "Tell me, if I owned a bar, and wanted to clean it up, how much would it take to get you to come work for me?" Dalton then walks out.

Movie Trivia:

Road House (1989) writer, David Lee Henry, also wrote *Out for Justice* (1991) starring Steven Seagal, and helped with the screen adaptation of R. Lance Hill's novel turned movie, *The Evil That Men Do* (1984) starring Charles Bronson.

About the Actor:

Patrick Swayze and Marshall Teague, who played Jimmy, became friends on the set of *Road House* (1989), and remained friends from then on.

"I don't know. I'm making this up as I go."

Harrison Ford as Indiana Jones – **Raiders of the Lost Ark (1981)**

Setting:

Indy learns from Sallah (John Rhys-Davies) that the Ark is being loaded on a truck headed for Cairo. He tells Sallah to get to Cairo and get transportation, and that he is going after the truck. Sallah asks, "How?" This was Indy's reply.

Movie Trivia:

Tag line for *Raiders of the Lost Ark* (1981): "Indiana Jones – the new hero from the creators of *Jaws* and *Star Wars*."

About the Actor:

Harrison Ford bruised his ribs during the scene where he is dragged behind the truck in *Raiders of the Lost Ark* (1981).

"Don't treat women like that!"

Nicolas Cage as Cameron Poe – **Con Air (1997)**

Setting:

Poe stops Johnny 'Johnny 23' Baca (Danny Trejo) from attacking guard Sally Bishop (Rachel Ticotin), and with each word, "treat-women-like-that" he smashes Johnny 23's head into the iron retaining fence inside the aircraft.

Movie Trivia:

Rachel Ticotin, who plays guard Sally Bishop, appeared in the hit television series *Lost* (2005-2006) as Captain Teresa Cortez in two episodes.

About the Actor:

Nicholas Cage's aunt, Talia Shire, is best known for her roles as Adrian in the *Rocky* movies and Connie Corleone in her brother's *Godfather* movies. She was nominated for an Oscar for both characters: Best Actress in a Leading Role for *Rocky* (1976), and Best Actress in a Supporting Role for *The Godfather Part II* (1974).

"Mental toughness is the ability to accept the fact that you're human and that you're gonna make mistakes, lots of them, all your life. And some of them are gonna hurt people that you love very badly. But you have the guts to accept the fact that you're imperfect and you don't let your mistakes crush you and keep you from trying to do the very best that you can."

Tom Laughlin as Billy Jack – **Billy Jack (1971)**

Setting:

Billy offers some advice to Martin (Stan Rice) after Barbara (Julie Webb) loses her baby to a horse riding accident. Martin replies, "A lot of good I could have done." Billy then tells him, "You sure could have. You could have gone inside and comforted that girl instead of sitting out here on the porch whining and feeling so sorry for yourself."

Movie Trivia:

Tom Laughlin and Delores Taylor's eleven year old daughter, Teresa, plays one of the students, Carol, and sings two self-written songs.

About the Actor:

Tom Laughlin's first starring role was in Robert Altman's 1957 film *The Delinquents* (1957), in which he played Scotty White.

"I'm afraid I'm a bad boy, ma'am."

Jean-Claude Van Damme as Eddie Lomax – **Desert Heat (1999)**

Setting:

After giving Lomax a key to bungalow five, where he can shower and clean up, the innkeeper, Mrs. Henry Howard (Priscilla Pointer), asks, "Young man? Have you been saved?" After the reply above, she tells him, "But it's never too late." Lomax turns and looks at her and replies, "I hope you're right."

Movie Trivia:

Desert Heat (1999) was directed by John G. Avildsen as Danny Mulroon. Avildsen won the 1977 Oscar for Best Director for *Rocky* (1976). It wasn't Avildsen's first time to work with Pat Morita either, since he also directed the first three *Karate Kid* movies.

About the Actor:

One of Jean-Claude Van Damme's first appearances was when he was cast as an extra in the film *Breakin'* (1984). He was an uncredited spectator in the first dance sequence.

"What do you think I'm gonna do? I'm gonna save the fuckin' day."

Nicolas Cage as Cameron Poe – **Con Air (1997)**

Setting:

Before Poe goes back to the airplane where his friend was left, he asks U.S. Marshal Vince Larkin (John Cusack) to tell his wife he loves her, and she's his humming bird, but he couldn't leave a fallen man behind. Larkin agrees, and then asks Poe, "What are you going to do for me?" The above is his reply.

Movie Trivia:

In the theatrical trailer, Poe is shown saying this quote, without the expletive, to Larkin over the radio on the plane, not where he actually says it in the movie.

About the Actor:

Nicolas Cage's cousin Jason Schwartzman played Ringo Star in an uncredited role in *Walk Hard: The Dewey Cox Story* (2007).

"I've heard that you're a low-down Yankee liar."

Alan Ladd as Shane – **Shane (1953)**

Setting:

Shane faces off with Jack Wilson (Jack Palance) and says, "So, you're Jack Wilson." Wilson replies, "What's that mean to you, Shane?" "I've heard about you," answers Shane. "What have you heard, Shane?" Wilson asks. After Shane tells him what he's heard, Wilson tells him to prove it and draws. Shane proves he's the fastest.

Movie Trivia:

Jack Palance was nominated for a 1954 Oscar for Best Actor in a Supporting Role for his performance as Jack Wilson in *Shane* (1953).

About the Actor:

In 1953, Alan Ladd won the Photoplay Award for Most Popular Male Star.

"Maybe later, when I put you to sleep."

Clive Owen as Smith – **Shoot 'Em Up (2007)**

Setting:

Smith's reply to Hertz (Paul Giamatti) when Hertz requests a story, one about the baby.

Movie Trivia:

Paul Giamatti plays the outlandish bad guy Hertz in *Shoot 'Em Up* (2007), but he is more known for serious roles in films such as *Sideways* (2004), *Cinderella Man* (2005), and *American Splendor* (2003). He obviously enjoyed hamming it up in *Shoot 'Em Up* (2007) with lines such as "Guns don't kill people. But they sure help."

About the Actor:

Clive Owen was born October 3, 1962, in Keresley, Coventry, Warwickshire, England, UK.

"Men are gonna get killed here today, Sue. And I'm gonna kill them."

Kevin Costner as Charley Waite – ***Open Range (2003)***

Setting:

Waite's comments to Sue Barlow (Annette Bening) before he heads off with Boss Spearman (Robert Duvall) to face Denton Baxter (Michael Gambon) and his henchmen.

Movie Trivia:

Even though *Open Range* (2003) was filmed in Alberta, Canada, the story was set in the 1800s of Montana.

About the Actor:

Kevin Costner is the singer in a band he founded called Kevin Costner and Modern West. The band played at the Historic Wilma Theater in author Alain Burrese's home town of Missoula, Montana, on July 31, 2009.

"I'm your huckleberry."

Val Kilmer as Doc Holliday – **Tombstone (1993)**

Setting:

Johnny Ringo (Michael Biehn) calls Wyatt Earp (Kurt Russell) out on the street, and Earp tells him, "Not gonna fight you, Ringo. There's no money in it." Ringo then yells out, "Don't any of you have the guts to play for blood?" Holliday then steps up and says the above and that it's just his game. Holliday also says "I'm your huckleberry" to Ringo when they meet for their final shoot-out near the end of the movie, when Ringo is expecting Earp.

Movie Trivia:

Kevin Jarre began as director, but was fired after filming Charlton Heston's scenes. Kurt Russell acted as director (unofficially) until the studio sent George P. Cosmatos to take over.

About the Actor:

Val Kilmer attended Chatsworth High School with Kevin Spacey and Mare Winningham.

"Before this war is over, I'm going to kill you."

Mel Gibson as Benjamin Martin – **The Patriot (2000)**

Setting:

After tricking Gen. Lord Charles Cornwallis (Tom Wilkinson) into exchanging his prisoners, Martin addresses Col. William Tavington (Jason Isaacs), who earlier in the film killed Martin's unarmed son. Tavington goads him on and says, "Why wait?" Martin keeps his composure and answers, "Soon."

Movie Trivia:

The Patriot (2000) was directed by Roland Emmerich. Emmerich also directed *Universal Soldier* (1992) and *Independence Day* (1996) among other action films.

About the Actor:

Mel Gibson was ranked #15 in *Premiere's* 2003 annual "Power 100" list. He was ranked #17 in 2002.

"Young warriors used to like to fight head-on. Old warriors like to wait, let their opponents expose the board, work themselves into a corner."

Steven Seagal as Lt. Jack Cole – **The Glimmer Man (1996)**

Setting:

Cole provides Det. Jim Campbell (Keenen Ivory Wayans) a lesson in chess and strategy from *The Art of War* by Sun Tzu in a bar after laying a trap for the bad guys. Later, Campbell repeats the lessons and says they should wait to enter a room full of bad guys. Cole tells him he listens well and doesn't know why he doesn't follow his own advice as he kicks the door in.

Movie Trivia:

Keenen Ivory Wayans, who played Detective Jim Campbell, once played Customer #1 on the popular television series *Cheers* (1982).

About the Actor:

Steven Seagal's mother, Patricia, was a medical technician.

"Lie down. How you doing? Guess you're doing all right. Behind ya. I'll get the car."

Eric Roberts as Alexander Grady – ***Best of the Best 2 (1993)***

Setting:

Alex Grady and Tommy Lee (Phillip Rhee) fight their way out of the casino/coliseum after the first confrontation with Brakus (Ralf Moeller) and Weldon (Wayne Newton). Alex drops a guy and says, "Lie down." He turns to Tommy who is still fighting to ask how he's doing, and seeing him kick butt, comments he's doing all right. He then gives him a final warning regarding the last guard as he heads for the car.

Movie Trivia:

Robert Radler directed the first two *Best of the Best* films and the last two *Substitute* films, *The Substitute 3: Winner Takes All* (1999) and *The Substitute: Failure Is Not an Option* (2001), both with Treat Williams.

About the Actor:

Eric Roberts and sister Julia Roberts appeared together in *Blood Red* (1989).

"I remember my grandfather used to take a chicken, cut its head off, put it on the ground and watch it run around. I see you again, I'll introduce you to my grandfather. Don't come back."

Brian Bosworth as Joe Huff/John Stone – **Stone Cold (1991)**

Setting:

Huff and the FBI Agents put the Bolivian (Paulo Tocha) on a plane after Stone was sent to bring back his tattooed ear to gang leader Chains (Lance Henriksen).

Movie Trivia:

Stone Cold (1991) was written by Walter Doniger who also shared an executive producer credit. Most of Doniger's work has been with television.

About the Actor:

Brian Bosworth sued the NFL for the right to wear number 44, the number he wore since a kid. He lost and had to wear number 55. He got in trouble numerous times for having the number 44 somewhere on his body.

"Are you crazy? Is that the problem?"

Kurt Russell as Jack Burton – **Big Trouble in Little China (1986)**

Setting:

Burton's comment when David Lo Pan (James Hong) questions him and Wang Chi (Dennis Dun) about Miao Yin (Suzee Pai), and tells them if they don't answer they will be brought to the hell where people are skinned alive.

Movie Trivia:

James Hong, who played David Lo Pan, has a very long list of movie and television credits, including the voice of Mr. Ping in *Kung Fu Panda* (2008).

About the Actor:

Kurt Russell had a bout with the flu and had a high temperature while filming *Big Trouble in Little China* (1986). He and John Carpenter joke about it in the commentary on the DVD.

"I never gave up my family. Never."

Jean-Claude Van Damme as Lyon Gaultier – **Lionheart (1990)**

Setting:

Gaultier's reply to the Adjutant (George McDaniel) when he is told, "Your brother is not my problem. Or yours anymore. You gave up your family when you joined the Legion." After Gaultier is told he'll have hard labor, he tells the Adjutant, "You're a real asshole."

Movie Trivia:

Lionheart (1990) was Sheldon Lettich's directorial debut. In addition to writing and directing *Lionheart* (1990), Lettich wrote *Bloodsport* (1987), starring Jean-Claude Van Damme, and also had a hand in writing *Rambo III* (1988), *Only the Strong* (1993), and *Legionnaire* (1998). He also directed, co-wrote, and co-produced *Double Impact* (1991) with Van Damme in a dual role.

About the Actor:

Jean-Claude Van Damme had a story credit in *Lionheart* (1990), it read "Story by Jean-Claude Van Damme."

"Okay. Who's next?"

Danny Glover as Lieutenant Mike Harrigan – **Predator 2 (1990)**

Setting:

After killing the Predator, Lt. Harrigan faces 10 Predators near the end of the film, prompting the same question without the expletive asked by Martin Riggs (Mel Gibson) in Danny Glover's earlier film, *Lethal Weapon* (1987).

Movie Trivia:

Kevin Peter Hall played the Predator in both the original *Predator* (1987) and *Predator 2* (1990).

About the Actor:

Danny Glover and Arnold Schwarzenegger are the only two actors to survive hand-to-hand battles with a Predator in the first two movies.

"For your sake I hope so, cause you mess with my brother, you mess with me."

Patrick Swayze as Truman Gates – **Next of Kin (1989)**

Setting:

Truman Gates confronts Joey (Adam Baldwin) after his brother, Briar Gates (Liam Neeson), shot up John Isabella's (Andreas Katsulas) place looking for who killed their younger brother, Gerald (Bill Paxton).

Movie Trivia:

Bill Paxton, as Gerald Gates, and Ben Stiller, in a serious role as Lawrence Isabella, are both killed in *Next of Kin* (1989).

About the Actor:

Patrick Swayze was a licensed pilot with an instrument rating.

"I do it real good you know. (Murtaugh replies, 'Do what?') When I was 19, I did a guy in Laos from 1000 yards out. A rifle shot in high wind. Maybe eight, or even ten guys in the world could've made that shot. It's the only thing I was ever good at."

Mel Gibson as Sergeant Martin Riggs – **Lethal Weapon (1987)**

Setting:

Riggs reveals a bit of his past to Murtaugh (Danny Glover) before leaving Murtaugh's house after dinner and discussing the Huntsaker case. Murtaugh's comment about making it through the next day without killing anyone prompted the disclosure.

Movie Trivia:

Richard Donner directed *Lethal Weapon* (1987). He also directed all three sequels and *The Goonies* (1985) among many other films.

About the Actor:

Mel Gibson and actor Geoffrey Rush were roommates in college.

"Yeah, I got a deal for you. Roll out from under that rock you're hiding under and I'll drive this truck up your ass."

Bruce Willis as John McClane – **Die Hard With a Vengeance (1995)**

Setting:

McClane is driving the rear dump truck and informs Simon (Jeremy Irons) over the radio that his men are dead and won't be joining him. Simon says, "John. In the back of the truck you're driving, there's thirteen billion worth of gold bullion. I wonder would a deal be out of the question?" This was McClane's response.

Movie Trivia:

A year before *Die Hard With a Vengeance* (1995), Jeremy Irons played the voice of the villain Scar in *The Lion King* (1994).

About the Actor:

Bruce Willis attended Penns Grove High School in his hometown.

"You wanna shoot me? Huh? Shoot me now. Shoot."

Phillip Rhee as Tommy Lee – **Best of the Best 2 (1993)**

Setting:

Bad guys attack Alex Grady (Eric Roberts), his son, Walter (Edan Gross), and Tommy Lee at Alex's home. When one is holding a gun to Tommy's head, Tommy performs a fancy Hapkido move that ends up with the gun still in the bad guy's hand, but pointing at the bad guy's own head. After saying the above, Tommy tosses the gun aside and drops the guy before going on to dispatch other bad guys.

Movie Trivia:

German bodybuilder, Ralf Moeller, who plays Brakus, appeared as Robert E. Howard's Conan in the short lived (22 episodes) television series *Conan* (1997).

About the Actor:

Phillip Rhee holds black belts in Tae Kwon Do, Hapkido, and Kendo.

"Anything that much fun, I think I'd rather do it myself."

Bruce Willis as Joe Hallenbeck – ***The Last Boy Scout (1991)***

Setting:

Hallenbeck's reply to Jimmy Dix (Damon Wayans) after he had been arguing with his daughter (Danielle Harris) and Dix tells him, "You know, for 50 bucks you could pay a guy to pull her fingernails out one by one."

Movie Trivia:

The Last Boy Scout (1991) was produced by Joel Silver, who's produced many action movies, including: *Commando* (1985), *Lethal Weapon* (1987), *Die Hard* (1988), *Road House* (1989), *Executive Decision* (1996), *The Matrix* (1999), and *Ninja Assassin* (2009) among many others.

About the Actor:

Bruce Willis, along with fellow tough guy actors Sylvester Stallone and Arnold Schwarzenegger, started the Planet Hollywood restaurant chain.

"I ain't wasting a good bullet to ease your pain, you son of a bitch."

Robert Duvall as Boss Spearman – **Open Range (2003)**

Setting:

Spearman's final words to the dying Denton Baxter (Michael Gambon) after changing his mind about putting a bullet into his head. He had just replied to Baxter calling him "nothing" by saying, "Yeah? Maybe so. But I'll still be breathing in another minute."

Movie Trivia:

Boss Spearman (Robert Duvall) calls Percy (Michael Jeter) "Old Man" in the film *Open Range* (2003), when Duvall was actually 21 years older than Jeter who was 51 at the time the movie was filmed.

About the Actor:

Robert Duvall has been married four times. Barbara Benjamin, 1964-1975; Gail Youngs, 1982-1986; Sharon Brophy, 1991-1996; and Luciana Pedraza, 2004-present.

"Not me. It's my job to handle life-and-death situations on a daily basis. It's what I do, and I'm very good at it. Now you can stand there and be the panicked, angry mob and blame him, me, and the government for getting you into this. But if you want to survive tonight, you need to save your energy and start working together."

Samuel L. Jackson as Neville Flynn – **Snakes on a Plane (2006)**

Setting:

Agent Flynn's speech after a passenger states, "Oh, Jesus Christ, we're all dead," upon learning that the snakes are on the plane due to the witness, Sean Jones (Nathan Phillips), going to testify against Eddie Kim (Byron Lawson).

Movie Trivia:

Snakes on a Plane (2006) was directed by David R. Ellis. Ellis appeared in *Rocky III* (1982) as an unnamed opponent.

About the Actor:

Samuel Jackson played Eddie Murphy's uncle in a sketch for Eddie Murphy's *Raw* (1987).

"The Japanese have a saying. 'Fix the problem, not the blame.' Find out what's fucked up and fix it. Nobody gets blamed. We're always after who fucked up. Their way's better."

Sean Connery as Capt. John Connor – **Rising Sun (1993)**

Setting:

Capt. Connor cuts off Lt. Webster Smith (Wesley Snipes) as he is saying, "The chief says we fucked up. He's blaming us for …"

Movie Trivia:

Rising Sun (1993) was based on the novel by Michael Crichton. Philip Kaufman, Michael Crichton, and Michael Backes wrote the screenplay.

About the Actor:

Sean Connery won an Oscar for Best Actor in a Supporting role for *The Untouchables* (1987) in 1988.

"You're no daisy. You're no daisy at all."

Val Kilmer as Doc Holliday – **Tombstone (1993)**

Setting:

Said to Johnny Ringo (Michael Biehn) after out drawing him and shooting him in the head. Holliday then kneels over Ringo's dead body and says, "Poor soul. You were just too high-strung." Wyatt Earp (Kurt Russell) comes running up and Holliday tells him, "I'm afraid the strain was more than he could bear." As Earp looks at Holliday with a puzzled look, Holiday tells him, "Oh, I wasn't quite as sick as I made out." And when Earp picks up the badge he'd given Holliday, who had placed it on the dead body of Ringo, Holliday says, "My hypocrisy goes only so far."

Movie Trivia:

Michael Biehn, who played Johnny Ringo, has appeared in numerous television and movie roles, including: *The Terminator* (1984), *Aliens* (1986), *Navy Seals* (1990), *K2* (1991), and *The Rock* (1996) among many others.

About the Actor:

Val Kilmer was married to Joanne Whalley from 1988 to 1996 when the two divorced.

"Yippie-kai-yay, motherfucker."

Bruce Willis as Lt. John McClane – **Die Hard 2 Die Harder (1990)**

Setting:

As Col. Stuart (William Sadler) knocks him off the plane's wing where they were fighting, McClane pulls a lever that opens the fuel tank and the plane starts spilling fuel. He reprises his famous line from the first movie as he takes out a lighter and ignites the fuel, ending the terrorists' short flight with a huge explosion.

Movie Trivia:

In 1990, William Sadler played bad guy Col. Stuart in *Die Hard 2 Die Harder* (1990), the bad guy Senator Vernon Trent in Steven Seagals's tough guy action flick, *Hard to Kill* (1990), and the character Frank Sutton in *The Hot Spot* (1990) starring Don Johnson.

About the Actor:

The yippie-kai-yay line was so popular in the first *Die Hard* (1988), Bruce Willis used it again in *Die Hard 2 Die Harder* (1990).

"One thing I learned from Dom is that nothing really matters unless you have a code."

Paul Walker as Brian O'Conner – ***Fast and Furious (2009)***

Setting:

O'Conner talks with Mia Toretto (Jordana Brewster) about her brother Dominic Toretto (Vin Diesel), right before Dominic discovers his girlfriend Letty (Michelle Rodriguez) was working undercover for O'Conner when she was murdered.

Movie Trivia:

Fast and Furious (2009) was directed by Justin Lin, who also directed the third installment of the franchise, *The Fast and the Furious: Tokyo Drift* (2006).

About the Actor:

Paul William Walker IV was born on September 12, 1973, in Glendale, California.

"A man has to be what he is, Joey."

Alan Ladd as Shane – **Shane (1953)**

Setting:

Shane's final speech to Joey (Brandon De Wilde) about why he won't be going back with him, which continues, "Can't break the mold. I tried it, and it didn't work for me… Joey, there's no living with a killing. There's no going back from one. Right or wrong, it's a brand, and a brand sticks. There's no going back." Shane tells the boy to go back to his parents and then rides off to the sound of one of the most famous of movie lines, "Shane! Shane! Come back!"

Movie Trivia:

The movie line, "Shane! Shane! Come back!" was voted as the #47 (out of 100) movie quote by the American Film Institute. The line was voted #69 of "The 100 Greatest Movie Lines" by *Premiere* in 2007.

About the Actor:

The role that helped make Alan Ladd's career was playing Philip Raven, a hitman with a conscience, in *This Gun for Hire* (1942).

"You know what, pal? What do you think that means? Nothin'. Not diddly shit. See, there were 160 cats on north block, and I didn't want to know 159 of them, which included you. What do you think about that?"

Nicolas Cage as Cameron Poe – **Con Air (1997)**

Setting:

Poe's reply to William 'Billy Bedlam' Bedford (Nick Chinlund) when confronted after the convicts take over the plane with, "I was on north block. I don't know you."

Movie Trivia:

The song "How Do I Live" was nominated for both an Oscar as Best Original Song and a Razzie as Worst Original Song. It did not win either award.

About the Actor:

Nicolas changed his name to Cage because he wanted to succeed on his own merits, and not because of his uncle Francis Ford Coppola.

"You're gonna die, son. Put it away."

Patrick Swayze as Jack Crews – **Black Dog (1998)**

Setting:

Crews' comment to Wes (Brian Vincent), as Earl (Randy Travis), Sonny (Gabriel Casseus), and Wes have a stand-off in the men's room as Crews looks on.

Movie Trivia:

Besides country music star, sometimes actor, Randy Travis, *Black Dog* (1998) also features rock legend, sometimes actor, Meat Loaf (Michael Lee Aday, born Marvin Lee Aday) as bad guy Red.

About the Actor:

Patrick Swayze's first professional appearance was as a dancer for Disney on Parade.

"In what remote corner of this country, no, of the entire goddamn planet, is there such a place where men really care about another and really love each other? Now you tell me where such a place is, and I promise you that I'll never hurt another human being as long as I live."

Tom Laughlin as Billy Jack – **Billy Jack (1971)**

Setting:

Billy questions Jean (Delores Taylor) when she attempts to stop him from going to seek revenge against Bernard Posner (David Roya) for killing Martin (Stan Rice). Billy then finds Bernard with a young girl, and after ordering her out of the room, takes revenge for not only Martin, but for when Bernard raped Jean.

Movie Trivia:

Delores Taylor, who plays Jean Roberts, is Tom Laughlin's wife. Their children also appear in the movie.

About the Actor:

Tom Laughlin and his wife Delores Taylor wrote *Billy Jack* (1971), and used the names Frank Christina and Teresa Christina (using the names of their children) for the credits.

"I've been shot plenty of times. I've never felt lucky about it."

Kurt Russell as Gabe Cash – ***Tango & Cash (1989)***

Setting:

Cash pushes Tango (Sylvester Stallone) out of the way of a gunman and takes a bullet through the arm. He tells Tango that it's a clean exit. This is his reply when Tango states, "You're lucky."

Movie Trivia:

Peter MacDonald said of the stunts in the movie, "What you try and do, if you're sensible, is make a stunt work in one take. You don't want to ask a stuntman to take a risk twice."

About the Actor:

Kurt Russell rode along with the Chicago Fire Dept.'s Squad 5 in preparation for his role in *Backdraft* (1991).

"One thought he was invincible. The other thought he could fly. They were both wrong."

Steven Seagal as John Hatcher – **Marked For Death (1990)**

Setting:

Hatcher's reply when he gets back to the car after trying to find out where Screwface (Basil Wallace) is located, and Max (Keith David) asks him what happened. Hatcher had shot Jimmy Fingers (Tony DiBenedetto) and replied to his "I'm a made man" comment with "God made men." The Jamaican Nesta (Victor Romero Evans) told Hatcher to find Screwface himself, after being knocked around by Hatcher, and then jumped out a window to his death.

Movie Trivia:

Rita Verreos, who played Marta in *Marked For Death* (1990), appeared in the reality series *Survivor: Fiji* (2007).

About the Actor:

Steven Seagal was the martial arts coordinator for *Marked For Death* (1990).

"Point it at the bad guys and shoot."

Bruce Willis as Joe Hallenbeck – **The Last Boy Scout (1991)**

Setting:

Hallenbeck is driving as he, Jimmy Dix (Damon Wayans), and his daughter, Darian (Danielle Harris), are being chased by bad guys that they just escaped from in the woods. Hallenbeck gives one of his guns to Dix, who asks, "What am I going to do with this?" This was Hallenbeck's reply.

Movie Trivia:

Noble Willingham played bad guy Sheldon 'Shelly' Marcone. Willingham appeared as C.D. Parker in 141 episodes of *Walker, Texas Ranger* (1993 – 1999) with tough guy Chuck Norris.

About the Actor:

Bruce Willis appeared in *Moonlighting* for four years: March 3, 1985 through May 14, 1989.

"I would if I slept."

Mel Gibson as Sergeant Martin Riggs – **Lethal Weapon (1987)**

Setting:

Riggs' answer to Murtaugh's question, "What do you do, sleep with that thing under your pillow?" Murtaugh asks the question after seeing the impressive shooting of Riggs at the firing range, just before Riggs shoots a smiley face in another target.

Movie Trivia:

Lethal Weapon (1987) was nominated for an Oscar in the Best Sound category (Les Fresholtz, Rick Alexander, Vern Poore, and Bill Nelson).

About the Actor:

Mel Gibson was the sixth of eleven children to parents Hutton and Ann Gibson.

"Hey, fuckhead. Yeah, you – fuckhead. Just one thing I got to know, you got any aspirins? I've had a bad fucking headache all day long."

Bruce Willis as John McClane – **Die Hard With a Vengeance (1995)**

Setting:

McClane and Carver (Samuel L. Jackson) are tied together on top of a giant bomb that Simon Gruber (Jeremy Irons) is using to blow up the ship and all the gold they stole. Gruber just told them that killing McClane was a little bonus. After McClane's question, Gruber tells him it's his lucky day, throws him a bottle of aspirin, and tells him to keep the bottle.

Movie Trivia:

Writer Jonathan Hensleigh was detained by the FBI because he knew extensive information about the Federal Gold Reserve in Downtown Manhattan.

About the Actor:

Bruce Willis was cast in the class production of *Cat on a Hot Tin Roof* while at Montclair State University.

"We did get you out. A lot of people died in the process. I just wondered how you felt about it."

Kurt Russell as Snake Plissken – **Escape From New York (1981)**

Setting:

The question Plissken asks the President (Donald Pleasence) after asking for a moment of his time after rescuing him.

Movie Trivia:

Donald Pleasence, who played the President, also starred in John Carpenter's *Halloween* (1978), and a number of its sequels, as Dr. Sam Loomis.

About the Actor:

Kurt Russell's character Snake Plissken was featured in a comic book, *John Carpenter's Snake Plissken Chronicles*, published by Crossgen comics.

"You're made for each other."

Patrick Swayze as Dalton – **Road House (1989)**

Setting:

Said to Tinker (John Young) after a stuffed polar bear falls on him and knocks him out during the final confrontation at Brad Wesley's (Ben Gazzara) house.

Movie Trivia:

Road House 2: Last Call (2006) was a straight to DVD release that had nothing to do with the original movie. The main character was supposed to have been Dalton's son, and Dalton had been murdered years before the happenings portrayed in the sequel.

About the Actor:

Patrick Swayze performed the song "Cliff's Edge" on the *Road House* (1989) soundtrack.

"Not yet."

Bruce Willis as Lt. John McClane – **Die Hard 2 Die Harder (1990)**

Setting:

Bad guy, General Ramon Esperanza (Franco Nero), opens the plane door and says, "Freedom." McClane punches him back into the plane and says the above. He then goes into this speech, "You're supposed to stay in your seat until the plane reaches the terminal. No frequent-flier mileage for you." When he's asked who he is by Esperanza, he replies, "A cop. Yeah, one of the good guys. You're one of the bad guys, and now that I got your sorry ass, I'm going to trade it for my wife."

Movie Trivia:

Franco Nero, who portrayed General Ramon Esperanza, was nominated for a Golden Globe award in 1968 for Most Promising Newcomer for *Camelot* (1967).

About the Actor:

Bruce Willis was cast in *Moonlighting* (1985 – 1989) by the series creator Glenn Gordon Caron.

"Old Jack always says, 'What the hell.'"

Kurt Russell as Jack Burton – **Big Trouble in Little China (1986)**

Setting:

Said to Thunder (Carter Wong) and David Lo Pan (James Hong) right before the final fight.

Movie Trivia:

Carter Wong, who played Thunder, was a very popular Chinese actor before appearing in *Big Trouble in Little China* (1986).

About the Actor:

The Best of Times (1986) starring Robin Williams and Kurt Russell was released in January, while *Big Trouble in Little China* (1986) was released in July of the same year.

To Be Continued...

INDEX

MOVIES

12 Rounds (2009) 70
Above the Law (1988) 52
Appaloosa (2008) 25, 46, 105
Best of the Best 2 (1993) 122, 130
Best of the Best 4: Without Warning (1998) 104
Big Trouble in Little China (1986) 19, 124, 150
Billy Jack (1971) 5, 31, 89, 113, 141
Black Dog (1998) 140
Bloodsport (1988) 27
The Bourne Identity (2002) 49
The Butcher (2007) 7, 32, 84
Con Air (1997) 94, 112, 115, 139
Damage (2009) 18, 83
A Dangerous Man (2009) 20, 72
Desert Heat (1999) 114
Die Hard (1988) 1
Die Hard 2 Die Harder (1990) 22, 69, 136, 149
Die Hard With a Vengeance (1995) 23, 90, 129, 146
Enter the Dragon (1973) 11, 40, 95
Escape From L.A. (1996) 73
Escape From New York (1981) 147
Eye of the Tiger (1986) 55
The Fast and the Furious (2001) 28
Fast and Furious (2009) 63, 137
The Glimmer Man (1996) 43, 76,100, 121
The Gunfighter (1950) 6
Heat (1986) 33, 79
A History of Violence (2005) 58
Jaguar Lives! (1979) 67
The Last Boy Scout (1991) 75, 103, 131, 144
Last Man Standing (1996) 45, 57
Lethal Weapon (1987) 53, 108, 128, 145
Lethal Weapon 2 (1989) 21, 71

Lionheart (1990)   125
Marked For Death (1990)   143
Merchant of Death (1997)   62, 107
The Negotiator (1998)   17
Nevada Smith (1966)   80
Next of Kin (1989)   127
Ninja Assassin (2009)   54
Open Range (2003)   34, 81, 118, 132
Passenger 57 (1992)   64, 97
Pat Garrett and Billy the Kid (1973)   12
The Patriot (2000)   44, 120
Predator 2 (1990)   126
Raiders of the Lost Ark (1981)   39, 111
Rising Sun (1993)   134
Road House (1989)   2, 26, 37, 51, 74,
                                                        101, 110, 148

Ronin (1998)   8, 47, 93, 98
The Rundown (2003)   59, 106
Shane (1953)   10, 66, 96, 116, 138
Sherlock Holmes (2009)   38
Shoot 'Em Up (2007)   65, 117
Shooter (2007)   35, 82
Showdown In Little Tokyo (1991)   48
Silverado (1985)   30
Snakes On A Plane (2006)   78, 133
Sniper (1993)   9, 50
Steel Dawn (1987)   29, 92
Stone Cold (1991)   24, 123
Stone Cold (2005)   13, 42, 68, 77, 99
The Substitute (1996)   85
The Substitute 3: Winner Takes All (1999)   56
Taken (2008, U.S. 2009)   61
Tango & Cash (1989)   36, 91, 142
They Live (1988)   15, 87
Tombstone (1993)   3, 41, 109, 119, 135
Under Siege (1992)   60
Under Siege 2: Dark Territory (1995)   4

The Untouchables (1987)   16, 86, 102
U.S. Marshals (1998)   14, 88

ACTORS

Austin, Steve   18, 83
Berenger, Tom   9, 50, 85
Bosworth, Brian   24, 123
Busey, Gary   55
Cage, Nicolas   94, 112, 115, 139
Cena, John   70
Connery, Sean   16, 86, 102, 134
Costner, Kevin   34, 118
Damon, Matt   49
De Niro, Robert   8, 47, 93, 98
Diesel, Vin   28, 63
Downey, Robert, Jr.   38
Duvall, Robert   81, 132
Elliott, Sam   26, 101
Ford, Harrison   39, 111
Gibson, Mel   21, 44, 53, 108, 120, 128, 145
Glover, Danny   30, 71, 126
Harris, Ed   25, 46
Jackson, Samuel L.   17, 23, 78, 133
Johnson, Dwayne   59, 106
Jones, Tommy Lee   14, 88
Keith, Brian   80
Kelly, Jim   40
Kilmer, Val   41, 119, 135
Kristofferson, Kris   12
Ladd, Alan   10, 66, 96, 116, 138
Laughlin, Tom   5, 31, 89, 113, 141
Lee, Bruce   11, 95
Lewis, Joe   67
Lundgren, Dolph   48
Mortensen, Viggo   58, 105

Neeson, Liam 61
Owen, Clive 65, 117
Pare, Michael 62, 107
Peck, Gregory 6
Piper, Roddy 15, 87
Rain 54
Reynolds, Burt 33, 79
Rhee, Phillip 104, 130
Roberts, Eric 7, 32, 84, 122
Russell, Kurt 3, 19, 36, 73, 91, 109, 124, 142, 147, 150

Seagal, Steven 4, 20, 43, 52, 60, 72, 76, 100, 121, 143
Selleck, Tom 13, 42, 68, 77, 99
Snipes, Wesley 64, 97
Swayze, Patrick 2, 29, 37, 51, 74, 92, 110, 127, 140, 148

Van Damme, Jean-Claude 114, 125
Wahlberg, Mark 35, 82
Walker, Paul 137
Whitaker, Forrest 27
Williams, Treat 56
Willis, Bruce 1, 22, 45, 57, 69, 75, 90, 103, 129, 131, 136, 144, 146, 149

ABOUT THE AUTHOR

Alain Burrese is the author of *Hard-Won Wisdom From The School Of Hard Knocks*, eight instructional DVDs on martial arts and self-defense, a thriller titled *Lost Conscience*, and the *Tough Guy Wisdom* series. He is currently working on additional titles to the *Tough Guy Wisdom* series, another novel, additional instructional DVDs, and several other projects. Alain's background includes serving as a paratrooper with the 82nd Airborne Division, a sniper instructor for the 2nd Infantry Division, living and training in Japan and South Korea where he earned a 4th degree black belt in the self-defense art of Hapkido, teaching, bodyguarding, speaking, mediating, practicing law, security, and various other positions throughout the years. He currently lives in Montana with his wife and daughter, and when not with them, he spends his time writing, teaching, speaking, and helping others resolve conflict. That, and of course, watching tough guy movies.

TOUGH GUY WISDOM SERIES

Tough Guy Wisdom
Tough Guy Wisdom III: Revenge of the Tough Guy

Future Volumes:

Tough Guy Wisdom: John Wayne vol. 1
Tough Guy Wisdom: John Wayne vol. 2
Tough Guy Wisdom: Clint Eastwood
Tough Guy Wisdom: Charles Bronson
Tough Guy Wisdom: Chuck Norris
Tough Guy Wisdom: Sylvester Stallone
Tough Guy Wisdom: Arnold Schwarzenegger
Tough Guy Wisdom: Rise of the Super Heroes
Tough Guy Wisdom IV
Tough Guy Wisdom V
Tough Guy Wisdom VI
Tough Guy Wisdom VII
Tough Guy Wisdom VIII …

www.ingramcontent.com/pod-product-compliance
Lightning Source LLC
Chambersburg PA
CBHW071535040426
42452CB00008B/1021